Leslie Armour

THE IDEA OF CANADA

AND THE CRISIS OF COMMUNITY

Steel Rail Publishing
Ottawa, Ontario

Steel Rail Educational Publishing
P.O. Box 4357 Station E
Ottawa, Ontario K1S-5B3

Steel Rail Publishing acknowledges support from the
Ontario Arts Council and the Canada Council.

Edited by Gail Dexter Lord
Cover and book design: Roslyn Tremblay, Ottawa
Cover illustration: Sue Ashley, Manotick, Ontario

Printed and bound in Canada by
Love Printing. Cloth cover bound by
Canadiana Book Binding, Ottawa.

Canadian Cataloguing in Publication Data

Armour, Leslie, 1931-
The Idea of Canada; and the crisis of community

Bibliography: p. 171-180

ISBN 0-88791-026-2 cloth
ISBN 0-88791-024-6 paperback

1. Philosophy, Canadian. 2. Regionalism — Canada.
3. Biculturalism — Canada. 4. Nationalism — Canada. I. Title.

FC158.A75   F1026.A75   971'.001   C81-090095-5

A note on the illustrations

Just as a people must sometimes look for ideas of itself so it must also sometimes look for images — images which will convey its sense of itself. Elections, wars and cultural causes call forth such images. If they are grasped honestly they often serve not only whatever end calls them forth but also call attention to the tensions which underlie the self-image especially when the artists have that talent which creates something which has the ring of truth. The posters assembled here all manage a kind of self-analysis and even critical commentary in the midst of an act of propaganda. Our thanks to the Public Archives of Canada, the Canadian Pacific Railway, Heritage Canada, the National Book Festival, the Royal Winnipeg Ballet, and the University of Winnipeg. *Cover illustration* — Symbolic muskoxen in a defence formation. Under attack from wolves, a herd forms a tight circle to protect the young.

Contents

Preface

This is intended to be a hopeful book: I want to argue that, though there is demonstrably a crisis of community in Canada, we have resources with which to meet it. The strength of our inherited cultures and of the fund of ideas which we have, sometimes painfully, retained is much greater than we are inclined to believe. Indeed, in a troubled world, we are probably much better placed than most groups of men and women and I think we owe it to all human beings to build on rather than destroy our inheritance. The problems are great but, still, I am more inclined to celebrate than to lament.

The crisis of community is not local: in Italy, it may be seen in waves of meaningless violence. In the Soviet Union, it emerges in the endless conflicts between the authorities and a curious spectrum of opponents ranging from civil rights activists to black marketeers and currency speculators. In Iran, Moslem fundamentalists collide with modernists presenting alternatives between which sensible men may find it hard to choose. In India, new government powers are demanded against the threat of 'disorder'. In Poland, the demand for 'independent' trade unions has a curious sound. In an economy specified by a central government, the right not to accept that specification is also the right not to accept the government. In New York, the crime rate continues to grow. The attempted assassination of a newly-elected American president seems almost normal.

It is not, of course, news that we live in a disorderly world, but everywhere the crisis seems to be a crisis of community, 'community' being whatever it is which can legitimize institutions. And even in the United States where, as a rule, institutions have not been looked upon with the Kafkaesque suspicions common enough in Europe, there has been a dramatic fall in public acceptance of public institutions. The basis of the crisis is technologies of a certain sort *combined with* forms of public organization which are increasingly impersonal, so that, more and more, men sense that 'the situation' is out of control. Men and women may seek (as in Iran) to re-awaken the past or (as in Poland) to usher in an as yet unstructured future; but they seem everywhere to seek a closer kind of association. When even Mr. Trudeau accepts that there is nothing he can do about inflation, or the bank rate, or the relative value of the dollar, other men may be pardoned for thinking that at least one of our institutions has escaped our ability to render it legitimate.

There is a *crisis* because one senses that the limits of tolerance are being approached — that an arms race controlled by no community may explode in an ultimate disaster, that an ever-expanding economy may run to the end of some indispensible resource or render the world uninhabitable, or that some wave of senseless violence may turn Rome into a desert. The situation here in Canada is interesting not because our crisis is worse — indeed it is not — but because some of the possibilities for solutions may well be clearer here. This book argues that the idea of an organic society, one in which the individual has not traditionally been pitted against his society but in which the individual and his society have been seen as a continuity in which neither is intelligible without the other, was deeply embedded in our beginnings, and has never been eradicated. We have grappled from the beginning with the idea of a plurality of communities which may, despite their plurality, legitimize some of the same institutions; and with the idea that, even where there are different institutions, they may express some common principles and some common strategies. We have often thought about the idea — though we have often worried about it too — that these common principles and strategies might embody a single nation.

Part of our challenge here will be to get the basic concepts straight — to distinguish the plurality of communities from the plurality of institutions, to separate and clarify the ideas of institution, state and nation. Failure to do so has frequently led Canadians to react regionally to problems which may require larger scale conclusions, to accept economic arrangements which may be at war with our stated objectives, and to suspect one another of malevolent designs because our actual designs have not been expressed clearly. These issues are examined against a background, much of it drawn from the philosophical tradition in Canada. One may ask why one should bother with that background. Chiefly, because to find a solution, one must depart, at least a little, from the most common patterns of philosophizing in the world around us.

In the contemporary world, the two most evident strands of political philosophy are a kind of individualist "contractarianism" of the sort found in the United States in the work of John Rawls; and the theory developed chiefly from the writings of Karl Marx — the theory that social and political systems are to be understood and planned against the background of a theory of history which makes technology and economic order paramount.

On Rawls's theory, human beings are rational agents and rational agents choose always to do the best they can to further their own interests. If they could choose freely and without knowing what position each would occupy in the society they jointly designed, however, each would choose that society in which the least advantaged would have most advantage, because each of us might turn out to be the least advantaged. An ideal society would be based on a contract intended to achieve this end, a social order which, in Rawls' view, attains as nearly as possible to our intuitive notions of fairness.

His proposal is a kind of idealization of what many people (though by no means all) in the United States have taken to be the American dream. It permits very great inequalities. (Rawls says he is not concerned with equality) on condition that those inequalities make the least advantaged better off than they would be with less inequality. Advantages and disadvantages have first of all to do with the availability of services and of material goods. Such a system may also accommodate certain intangibles such as one's sense of well-being. It certainly accommodates the desire for freedom. Indeed, Rawls makes this paramount: one should choose that system which maximizes the freedom of the participants for, after all, the system is designed to optimize one's chances of acting so as to further one's own interests. But it cannot include certain other intangibles. It cannot weigh the value of being or not being in a society in which everyone pursues his own interests rather than the common good — for Rawls simply supposes that rationality consists of pursuing one's own interests. It also cannot include the value of equality. Most of all, of course, the system cannot accommodate whatever is no one's particular interest. That may well include the whole of the future after the time at which everyone now living is dead — and that bears heavily on our concerns about the environment. And what of the interests of those already dead but who devoted their lives to building the world in which we live? Is there no obligation not to violate their ideals?

On Rawls's view, if men did not know when they would be born, they would value social continuity. In the real world, of course, men do know what position they will probably occupy in the societies they plan, and those who accept the pursuit of self-interest as legitimate do pursue their self interest on that basis rather than on the basis that one should plan the best world for the most disadvantaged. If their behaviour is, on Rawls's view, rational, how shall we argue against them? For while Rawls's theory reflects on and seeks to improve a view of the world which has given us much that many of us enjoy, it has also given us slums, race-riots, and the cold war. It is a world view that makes a principle or a postulate of the individualism which expresses the isolation of men from each other and which seems typical of the "crisis of community."

The cultural balance

National Book Festival & Public Archives of Canada (C2776)

Gilles Robert, 1979

Will the pile topple? The Canada Council's National Book Festival began in hope — and a little uncertainty. Clearly, we have the materials of a culture. But given the hazards, can we make it through without tripping?

FESTIVAL NATIONAL DU LIVRE

J'AIME NOS LIVRES.

The alternative presented by Marxist theorists associated with much of the world outside the capitalist sphere envisages history as, in outline, pre-ordained. One can speed it up or slow it down, but we must move through the crises of capitalism to a world in which justice will, despite Rawls, include a measure of equality and towards a world in which, again despite Rawls, men will pursue not their self-interest but their joint interest. The important thing is to speed history up so as to minimize the extent and time of the suffering which lies between us and the classless society. This theory does overcome the unconcern with social continuity and mutual relationships which Rawls's theory proposes. Its problems arise because, in order to get to the goal in a reasonable time, one must have a substantial measure of ideological order. In the ordinary way, most men are victims of ideologies and misunderstandings characteristic of the capitalist world. They are shot through with aims and desires which arise only because they are victims of the system. They must therefore be led by those who know, those who have overcome the misimpressions, those who have developed the appropriate class consciousness. It is therefore important to maintain a single ideology but also difficult to do so, especially in a world in which ideas travel with great facility. I do not know just how Marx himself would have responded to all this, and I shall discuss the details of his theory at some length in Chapter 4. But those who have power and think of themselves as Marxists have generally resorted to the Gulag.

Between the Gulag and the Holiday Inn, of course, all sensible men will choose the Holiday Inn. But in a world where everyone pursues his own interest, it may be to no one's interest to displace enough of his resources to run the National Research Council of Canada in an effective way or, indeed, to enquire into how societies can be and should be run. The future may belong to Moscow. For a poor man in New York, a state-subsidized apartment in Omsk with good free medical care may seem better than poverty in the Bronx.

This book, however, is dedicated to the notion that between these two theories there lie other options, and that they make particularly good sense in Canada. The idea of a society at once organic and pluralistic has very old roots in Canada. A society is organic if the parts work together to form an intelligible whole in which each has a unique place. I do not mean to use "organic" as a biological metaphor but in the more fundamental sense given in the *Oxford English Dictionary*: "pertaining to or characterized by systematic connection or co-ordination of parts in one whole." The idea of an organic society is the idea of a society in which mutual interest, mutual dependence and a common good which surpasses all individuals have a place. Such a society may also be pluralistic. For the one whole may be so organized as to serve a variety of cultures, communities and ways of life.

What we need is a theory which accounts for the importance of history and tradition and yet which tells us how to organize a society in which the future is open, and in which there is no need to impose a single ideology. In the middle part of this book, I shall draw on a variety of Canadian theorists, French and English, Catholic and Protestant, recent and distant from us. Some may seem radical, like John Clark Murray; and others, rather conservative, like Charles de Koninck. But, it is as well to remember that, if one seeks the space between Rawls and Marx, the space between the liberal individualist and the systematic collectivist, the received categories will not make much sense.

The context, however, is important. One must try to sense just what problems constitute our crisis of community. In the first part of the book, I shall explore notions of political order, community, and culture. Since our problems seem to arise in the context of a conflict between our inherited notions of an organic society and our confrontations with the technologically-based individualism associated with the economies of the contemporary west, I shall begin the theoretical discussion in Part II with the critiques of enlightenment individualism (and its associated modes of rationality) found in the writings of Hegel, Marx and Freud. It is because their critiques seem inadequate to *our* situation that I shall draw on specific elements in our own Canadian tradition. This book does not propose to provide a history of that tradition. That history exists elsewhere: Elizabeth Trott and I have tried to document that tradition for English Canada, and Yvan Lamonde and Roland Houde have done so for French Canada. The notes and bibliography provide references to these and other relevant works.

I shall simply draw freely on what I need.

Though it has a specific task and context, this is a work of philosophy. I see no contradiction between the two. Philosophy is concerned with the giving and taking of reasons, or the establishment of the impossibility of giving and taking reasons about the most basic questions concerning the world and human life. It tends to arise (as in ancient Greece, or the Europe of the high middle ages or the Germany of the late eighteenth and early nineteenth centuries) when there is a clash of intuitions about such things and when, therefore, someone's intuitions *must* be replaced by reasons. Because we have had a plurality of cultures, because we retained some ancient convictions in the face of the enlightenment, and because we inherited religious traditions (especially Catholic and Presbyterian) in which the giving and taking of reasons was considered important, philosophy has always been a serious industry in Canada.

The arguments have to be brought back now and then to the actual situations which give rise to the conflicts of intuitions if the whole enterprise is not to disappear into Cloud-Cuckoo-Land. This book, is therefore, a small sortie undertaken, at least, in an effort to find out where the front line is in our own affairs. Philosophy, admittedly, rather quickly becomes technical. Most people remember Bertrand Russell for his pacificism or his views on marriage or on morals, or his witty asides on the history of philosophy; but he himself (in a B.B.C. broadcast) said that his greatest contribution to philosophy was his theory of definite descriptions, a theory intended to solve a logical problem which most people would not even notice in their ordinary affairs. The Sartre of popular imagination exchanged profundities about the meaning of life while he sat through the night with his friends in a café adjoining what has just become La Place du Québec; but the other Sartre also spent his mornings there with pen and paper trying to decide how to express the notion that existence precedes essence. From the tree of Porphyry to Willard Quine's *New Foundations for Mathematical Logic*, philosophers have distinguished, made precise, even niggled about matters which seem remote from men and life.

I have no objection to this. If I were asked to justify my philosophical life I would, I suppose, point (though with some trepidation) to the theory of specific exclusion reference in *Logic and Reality* or to some (as I thought) improvements which I made on Collingwood's theory of truth in *The Concept of Truth*. And if I were asked what gave me most personal pleasure in philosophy, I would point to some of my papers in philosophical theology which were published in Scotland or Sweden or Australia in small journals for those determined souls who still pursue the logical conundrums with which philosophers have dared to confront the gods since classical antiquity. For this activity seems to sum up that mixture of rationality and determined imprudence which makes human beings interesting.

Nonetheless, I would insist that we must sometimes journey to the source of our problems and that we must, then, try to make our findings intelligible to our fellow citizens. In so doing, the problem is not about how to write down to this larger audience but how to write *up* to it. For every reader of this book has had a lifetime of experience far more complex than the philosophical ideas he will find here, and his experience of his community will suggest a logical tangle of very great proportions. The philosophical theory must be simpler than the experience — for it is meant to help in ordering that experience.

One must, I admit, try to avoid strange terminology and explain the terminology one does use (again, I would refer to the notes at the back of this book) and one must stop short of certain logical complications. In any event, *this* book seeks only to introduce some problems and some concepts and theories and to suggest how they might be applied. In such matters the reader must make up his own mind. It is of no importance whether he agrees with me or not; for he may well be able to use the materials I have provided to create a better theory of his own.

To make that possible, a book like this *must* stop short of some logical complications. I hope to deal with what is avoided here in two other books. One of them, tentatively called *The Metaphysics of Community*, exists in a substantial draft. It will contain my own further theorizing and use the Canadian material in just the way that a French philospher would use his own philosophical tradition or an American philosopher would use his. The second book will be called (I think) *Social Continuity and the Idea of the Nation in Canada* and will provide more historical material. It will also explore at more depth the ideas of social continuity and nationhood which are raised here.

These works arise out of a project funded by the Social Sciences and Humanities Research Council of Canada. This book might be thought of as an interim report on that project, but it addresses specific contemporary problems and it is intended primarily for a general audience. I shall do my very best in the forthcoming books to address a general audience, too, but, in those books, I shall try to lead that audience onto the ground more generally occupied by scholars. This book is not the one intended by the Council's project, yet I must take this opportunity to thank its staff for their very great help.

This book posed its own problems and required its own kind of effort, and it was made possible by a generous grant from the Ontario Arts Council intended to support writers under a programme which has done much for writing and publishing in Ontario, and I extend my heartfelt thanks to that Council, too.

It should be emphasized that no other person may want to be associated with the views expressed here, but many people deserve thanks. The research which went into *The Faces of Reason* is also a crucial part of the background of this book and I must again, thank Dr. Elizabeth Trott with whom I did that research over nearly a decade. Many of my students of recent years, at the University of Ottawa and at The Cleveland State University have played crucial roles in developing my ideas and thanks are particularly due to Brenda and Tom Tokmenko, Roger Pryor, Linda Kabat, C.P. Singh, Hal Mowat, and Mimi Singh.

Thanks are also due to many senior members of the profession: to Hilton Page, Peter Smale, Steven Burns, Morton Paterson, A. H. Johnson, Yvan Lamonde, Louise Marcil-Lacoste, Roland Houde, Brian Keenan, and many others who have kept alive my interest in Canadian philosophy.

Roselyne Revel, my principal assistant on the current Social Sciences and Humanities Research Council project has, of course, played a special role. Her patient questioning has done much to shape my ideas and she has rekindled my interest in P.J. Proudhon, the printer-philosopher who lived a life which, as a young newspaperman, I imagined for myself. (She has also put up with my French for the last two-and-one-half years!)

The members of the Steel Rail Publishing co-operative encouraged me to write the book and, without that encouragement, I am sure it would not have been written. Without the work of their editor, Gail Dexter Lord, it would have been much less accessible.

Finally, but by no means least, without Diana Armour neither this nor any of my books could have been written. Readers cannot guess how much confusion they have been spared by her services as unofficial editor, but I am aware of the extent to which all my tasks would be rendered harder without her.

No part of this book has appeared in print before. But parts of Chapter 6 were read to the Canadian Philosophical Association in Saskatoon at the Learned Societies of Canada meetings of 1979; parts of Chapter 7 were an invited address to the Atlantic Philosophical Association in October, 1979; and parts of Chapter 8 were read at the University of Winnipeg in 1978, in a different form at Carleton University later that same year and in a still different form at the Conference on Canadian Philosophy at the University of Ottawa early in 1979. My thanks to all those who listened and made suggestions and to the organizations and universities concerned.

Ottawa, Canada
May, 1981

Part I

Posing the Problems

Chapter 1

The Paradoxes of Regionalism

*T*he existence of Canada has always excited wonder. The Americans carefully provided for its inclusion when they wrote the early drafts of their constitution. The impulse was not ungenerous and it was a long walk to Quebec City. The revolutionaries were a little surprised when they were not invited in to tea. Possible explanations included natural conservatism, greed, stupidity and the innate wickedness of the United Empire Loyalists. Above all, Americans tended to blame Canada on the machinations of the British. If Pierre Berton is right in surmising that there might not now be a Canada if the war of 1812 had not occurred, the British may deserve the blame, though in a rather indirect way.

Not so long afterwards, however, Britons like Lord Durham had little hope that Canada could survive unless its inhabitants smartened up, spoke English, and learned to take the Empire more seriously. Even John Stuart Mill agreed that a country with more than one language was a shaky proposition. Nor, in fact, did the British have much interest in further machinations to keep Canada in existence. As John Ewart remarked, "In the 1840s, the United Kingdom adopted free trade; threw open her colonies to traffic with foreign nations; lost her interest, therefore, in Canada; and told her (in Tennyson's phrase) to 'cut the cords and go'."

It cannot really be said that the continued existence of the country has been less surprising to people at home. We can ignore those who have actively hoped for the country's demise and concentrate on its friends. But they include George Grant who appeared to believe that the country was so feeble that the political defeat of John Diefenbaker justified a lament. He had a point. Diefenbaker represented a basic set of values which were national in scope (unlike other Tories, he *could* win support in Quebec) and which had their roots in an ordered society with a sense of the common good. Grant blamed Diefenbaker's failure to govern in some measure on actual and overt pressure from the Americans but in much larger measure on the fact that, in a society dominated by an industrial technology and embraced in a network of social phenomena which comprised what had become the "Great Lakes culture," such values had little chance of finding a workable expression. Thus Diefenbaker symbolized our separateness and the symbol was closely related to the reality it symbolized. One must normally be dead in order to be lamented, but it was Grant's thesis that we continued on, not so much resurrected as reactivated, like Frankenstein's monster. The future of such an existence is not bright.

We may also number amongst our gloomy friends the late Donald Creighton who believed that the explanation for our existence must depend upon the power of the St. Lawrence to create the opportunities which generated a commercial empire. That empire eventually thrust itself across the Great Lakes and ultimately to the Pacific. But this, even if it is an explanation, is certainly a gloomy one. For the relative and marginal advantage of access to water began to decline with the arrival of the railway. Though it is far from nil, is has declined still further with the development of high technology. In any case, the water stops at Thunder Bay and the thrust toward the Empire of the St. Lawrence has been vastly weakened by commercial and industrial networks which spread across North America and the world. As we shake off our memories of the old order, Creighton's Canada, as Creighton himself so strongly feared, appears an unlikely candidate for survival.

Anyone who reads the newspapers can hardly be faulted for thinking that, if Grant and Creighton were not right, then some other thesis along the same lines must be forthcoming. One of every two French-speaking Québécois who voted in René Lévesque's referendum was willing to negotiate for "sovereignty association." On the eve of a national constitutional conference, the government of British Columbia dropped leaflets on the doorsteps of its constituents explaining how British Columbia had been squeezed to provide a market for industry in central Canada. A B.C. television talk show host recently told a Cabinet Minister that he seemed "quite nice for an Ontarian". Alberta has been claiming the right — moral, political, and legal — to dispose of its own oil without interference from the federal government. Newfoundland has demanded control not only of its oil but of its fish as well.

The right to work on one side or the other of the Ottawa River may depend upon which province one normally lives in — and the two provinces negotiate about the matter much as if they were Germans and Frenchmen in the days before the Common Market.

The right to attend an English school in Quebec is denied to those whose parents did not attend English schools in Quebec, thus restoring hereditary privilege in a French jurisdiction for what may well be the first time since the Revolution. Proposals to give the provinces jurisdiction over 'family' law could mean that anyone who crosses a provincial line might acquire, or lose, a wife as well as a large and complex set of responsibilities.

As the jurisdictions pull apart, those who live in one part of the country find that even information about other parts of the country is difficult to come by, and information about Canadian involvements abroad is virtually impossible to discover. To many Canadians, Ottawa seems curious and distant, the location of political manipulations as little intelligible as those in Sofia or Reykjavik — a place nowhere near as homey as Ames, Iowa, or whatever centre of civilization is the source of tonight's chatty little film clip borrowed from NBC or CBS. The national news on our radio and television networks is nightly divided into French and English jurisdictions, each of which creates its own view of the world from points deep in the provinces without consulting the other. The international news in our newspapers is chiefly gathered by American, British and French agencies, and reflects the perspectives and interests of the gatherers. New claims to provincial jurisdiction over electronic communications might provide still more opportunities to evade all word of the doings of other Canadians.

Immediately behind these commonplaces are two profound puzzles. The first is that the fragmentation mainly takes the form of regionalism but that, though the regionalist thrust is a response to deep, old, and real injustices, the forms which it takes seem likely to make the problems worse and, indeed, to be self-defeating. The second is that though there has always been a scramble to 'explain' Canada, there is an identifiable and historical culture, and even some sociological data to show that there is much more to it than the confrontation of ancient pecksniffing Tories with modern, upstart, Americanized Liberals.

Everyone knows it pays to speak English even if one lives in Quebec. Despite recent trends toward equality, there are many opportunities to make contacts and get ahead which simply do not exist if one's only language is French. At best, it has only just begun to pay to learn French if you are English and that change, if it is a permanent one, is evidently the result of tremendous political pressure. Indeed, one need only stop a random selection of men and women on the street in Victoria or Regina to learn that discrimination exists. Ask first how the respondents would feel if no one would speak to them in English in Montreal. Then ask whether a Québécois has the right to expect that he will be spoken to in French in Victoria or in Regina.

Everyone grasps that raw materials are frequently (in some cases mainly) sold on world markets for which there is a competitive (often depressed) price while manufactured goods are most often protected by tariffs. The result has been very often that a farmer, a logger, a miner or a fisherman in Nova Scotia, Saskatchewan or British Columbia must sell what he produces, or have it sold for him, at a price over which he has no control — a price which is quite often the lowest price in the world. A man who makes tractors, or chain saws, or engines for fishing boats in Quebec or Ontario, by contrast, may be able to sell his goods at a price which is far from the lowest in the world. It stings to buy at the top and sell at the bottom.

Everyone in Ontario understands the importance of keeping oil prices at a level which will 'keep our industry profitable.' But the same people would find it strange if the price of Ontario tractors were fixed well below world prices in order to 'keep our grain industry competitive.' Of course, there are differences. Oil producers are currently rich and tractor makers have their backs to the wall. But historically there has been a tendency to regard raw materials as something to be controlled for the public good and the factories of central Canada as something which God and the free enterprise system intended to be run for the benefit of their private owners. It is not clear that this is consistent. It is certain that it is unjust.

It is as well to remember that these hoary complaints themselves pale into insignificance beside the injustices wreaked on native peoples — whose societies may have been damaged in many cases beyond repair — or on immigrant groups such as the Doukhobors many of whose members have been bullied into assimilation while their central culture has fallen into the hands of an extremist sub-sect. A recent report compiled for the Canadian Broadcasting Corporation suggested that there has been a marked movement of native people in the last decade into the cities where scarcely one in three has a job and where the juvenile delinquency rate is three times as high amongst them as it is for the population of European origin, while the adult crime rate is seven times as high. For native peoples the crisis of community is out in the open.

The remedy proposed for the problem of the Francophone is linguistic protection. In order to keep the power necessary to provide that protection, the Parti Québécois has been opposed to the entrenchment of language rights in the federal constitution. It is certainly true that the protection offered by the language laws has been effective in lessening the pressure on the French language in Quebec. It has also increased the confidence of French speakers and, indeed, created a certain élan in the French culture.

But consider the longer term and the larger context. Serious concern has been expressed in France recently about the strength of the language in the places in which it confronts other languages — Switzerland, Belgium and Canada in particular. Why are these places in which languages and cultures confront each other important? Largely because the possibility of carrying on a professional or intellectual life in French depends on there being others outside who take the trouble to learn French and ensure, in fact, that what is expressed in French is heard in the world. A recent study undertaken by the Quebec government confirms the peril: the document examined 4,846 works published by researchers at the University of Montreal, Laval University and five Quebec research institutions, and found that 71% were written in English. Fifty-six percent of the papers read at conferences by the same researchers were also in English.

Suppose you are a brain surgeon or a civil engineer. If you make important contributions to your field, you want them known. Even if you don't, you need to know what's going on in the rest of the world. You would look silly if someone discovered a design flaw in the kind of bridge you are creating and you didn't know about it until your bridge fell down. If you are a serious brain surgeon, you won't take a chance on not knowing what's going on in the world. So if you speak French, you will either rely on others who make contact across the language line or you will learn English. But if all the brain surgeons learn English and all the basic literature is in English, brain surgery will eventually be conducted in English. Professional translators may fill the gap to a very limited extent. But one really needs people who know what they are talking about — other professionals who form a natural 'interface.'

If there is a substantial population which needs to learn French but normally works in its own language, there is a natural 'interface' composed of those people together with those French speakers who do learn English but who also continue to work in their own language because their colleagues generally do. This natural 'interface' is provided in countries like Belgium and Switzerland and, increasingly, as a result of public sentiment and the government policies which that sentiment provokes, in Canada. A national language charter would provide substantial backing for that movement.

The isolation of French in Quebec would, from that perspective, be a disaster, more so if it was accompanied by the gradual decline of the English-speaking population. One need only look at France to see what the result might be. In France the regional languages — 'les langues d'Oc,' Breton, Corsican, Basque, Catalan and Flemish — are spoken every day by five million people. Ten million understand them. Eight million people — twice the French-speaking population of Quebec — are thought to understand one of 'les langues d'Oc' (Limousin, Auvergnat, Gascon, Languedocien or Provençal), and two million speak one of them regularly. These languages did not die. But they have been confined to special regions. Professional life and the affairs of big business are rarely carried on in them. Languages are very persistent. But they can also be by-passed as vehicles for serious intellectual and professional life. For them to survive in the large world, someone outside must continue to take them seriously.

It seems certain that some special protection for French in Quebec is necessary, including no doubt rules which specify that immigrants from outside Canada must expect to learn French and have their children educated in French-language schools. But that need not interfere with a national language charter which would guarantee the continued existence of the English-speaking culture and the continued meeting of the cultures, as well as the right of Canadians from other parts of Canada (including immigrants who are already citizens) to have their children educated in English. It is not enough that French should just survive.

The renaissance of Québécois culture in Quebec has been centred on Montreal. It takes a large city to sustain a major culture. But Montreal has been possible only as an entrepôt which functions as a financial and commercial centre for a country much bigger than Quebec. There are smaller countries than an independent Quebec would be — Finland, Denmark, and Iceland for example. But Helsinki, Copenhagen and Reykjavik are not the size of Montreal. Without other major changes of a cultural and institutional kind, a much reduced Montreal would mean the erosion of the base on which its present activities are built. It is difficult to imagine enough change coming about quickly enough to accommodate a large reduction in size without disaster.

The demoralizing effect of dismantling such a city and dispersing a significant part (even, say twenty percent) of its population scarcely bears thinking about. But the decline of institutions such as the Montreal stock exchange and the dispersal of financial activity already suggests the need for dramatic action on a national basis to keep these things functioning. Regionalist solutions are surely incapable of doing so. Even if one suspects powerful Torontonians of actively encouraging such a disaster, one must grasp the fact that only a national policy can create a balance between the historic rivals.

The paradox is this: existing injustices and threats to the continuance of French-Canadian culture stimulate regionalist responses. But regionalist responses could only make the situation worse. The future of French-Canadian culture in North America is almost certainly tied to the future of Canadian federalism.

The other injustices provoke paradoxes which are at least analagous. Suppose one responds to the traditional problem of high prices for manufactured goods made in central Canada and low prices for raw materials found east and west of the centre by abolishing all protection of Canadian industry. Then, evidently, a weakened economy in central Canada will be a poor market for whatever is produced in the Maritimes and the West. That economy will also be unable to supply traditional manufactured goods. The domestic market is important for most of our major producers of raw materials, from natural gas to fish. To get access to stable markets, the Maritime and western provinces would have to enter some other economic union. If Albertans think that they are 'used' as a captive market and kept in bondage, they might look at Montana or Idaho. The centralizing pull of a much more powerful economy is not less.

Albertans might get rich momentarily from control of their own oil. But oil is a declining resource and, even if it were not, the world must soon convert from it. The long-term effects of pollution from the combustion of fossil fuel are simply unacceptable. The probability is that either atomic fusion (a process which creates neither radiation hazard nor waste disposal problems) or solar power beamed from outer space will prove both more acceptable and much cheaper, and the oil industry will become obsolete. Indeed, before such solutions become general, there is certain to be a major development of power sources which lie closer to our present technology: tidal and wave power will generate electricity along our coasts, electricity not needed at off-peak times will be used to free hydrogen (atomically, the dominant component of water), and earth-bound solar generators will become more efficient. The University of Toronto's engineering school is a major centre of hydrogen research and the use of off-peak electricity from

CPR Archives (14416)   M. Leone Bracker, 1931

Technology, symbolically always the railway, re-organized geography — but it not only brought the world to your door, it might take away your father or your brother, too. It created new regions and broke down old regionalisms.

Ontario's electrical generators to separate hydrogen — a fuel capable of replacing existing fossil fuels in many applications — could well restore Ontario's industrial advantage.

The Alberta government has recognized for some time that it must prepare for a different future. Many Albertans understand that their problem, in reality, is to create a society diversified enough to provide stability and a reasonable choice of occupations for its population. Clearly, for that, one will need diversified industry and a market in which one can exercise some influence on the patterns of trade. Just as one must try to imagine an independent Quebec exercising influence on a vast North American culture run from Washington, so one must try to imagine an Alberta, which has become stronger by weakening the federation of which it is a part, influencing either a floundering Canadian economy or a not very much interested American one. Of course, it goes without saying that an automobile factory in Ontario is as much a resource as an oil well in Alberta, and that justice cannot be achieved until both are treated as factors that must be used to the national advantage.

But the injustices cut deeper. They have to do with the fact that the quality of life is not the same everywhere in the country, and that the miseries of some are turned to the advantage of others. But the disparities take place within regions as well as between them: cheap fish makes for rich canners, cheap timber enriches furniture manufacturers, a glut of pumpkins may pay off for grocers.

Our ability to cope with these problems is surely weakened rather than strengthened by regionalist thrusts. This is true, as well, for the problems of native peoples. Their immediate conflicts are with provincial or territorial jurisdictions in which their efforts to develop their own cultures in ways which will enable them to maintain a measure of independence, together with a chance to share in some of the advantages of the surrounding cultures, collide with expanding technology and commercial practice. It is only by creating a body of disinterested public opinion that they can hope to withstand the pressures. But disinterest requires a certain distance. A man in Nova Scotia can look at Indian land claims in the Yukon with quite different emotions than those which are apt to be aroused in a Yukoner or even in a British Columbian who finds his own conflicts analagous to those under review.

In any case, to have a country with a reasonable distribution of opportunity and comfort we need considerable redistribution of people and skills, for we must have substantially more diversification of activities in every region except the southern portion of two central provinces. That redistribution might be achieved on a continental basis. But the willingness to undertake it depends upon the existence of a culture with sufficient unity and an appropriate outlook on the future. Beneath the surface conflicts, is anything there? What links us in a way which makes one think that the appropriate responses are even possible, let alone likely?

In the earliest phases, the most influential groups of immigrants were French, Scots, and United Empire Loyalists. Their influence has remained critical. Though it was modified by waves of English and Irish immigrants and then by immigrants from Western Europe, the communalist thrust of these groups was reinforced by very substantial migration from Eastern Europe. The French, the Scots, and the United Empire Loyalists all tended dominantly toward an organic view of society. The French were here before the Revolution, resisted it (though it had a not altogether unfriendly reception from what there was of the press), and continued their traditional social order. The Scots were often clannish, resistant to the new orders which had displaced them at home, and fiercely loyal to their own traditions. The United Empire Loyalists included a good many men and women who specifically rejected the new individualism even if, as is always the case with those who flee some new regime, they also included a good many men and women who wanted to defend entrenched privilege or to take advantage of the rewards which the 'other side' offered.

The intellectual life in philosophy and letters overwhelmingly endorsed and expanded the belief in an organic society that these three groups had in common. It is true that this culture is spread unevenly, but historical processes have tended to keep it from being obliterated. Alberta attracted large numbers of Americans from the Dakotas, but they were balanced by migrations from eastern Europe of peoples relatively little touched by the industrial revolution. British Columbia from the beginning was more strongly English in outlook, but the movement of Ontarians westward and later substantial movements from the prairies continued to give it some Canadian flavour.

There is a little sociological data to show that a set of social attitudes distinctively Canadian actually persisted at least into the very recent past, though the data also tends to show a culture under great pressure and to underline the notion of a crisis of community. A study reported in 1973 by Gordon F.N. Fearn examined a number of characteristics in which respondents from across Canada were compared with Americans and Englishmen who had responded in a slightly earlier study to the same questions. The study was based on British and American data from 1968 and

Canadian data from 1970. There was a substantial distribution across regions and amongst ethnic groups, but very few French-speaking persons responded. There is a good deal of other information, however, to suggest that a better representation of Francophones would have strengthened the tendency of the study to reveal an organic society still at work.

The Canadians who responded showed a greater degree of family solidarity than the Americans and less than the Englishmen, though their children seemed less independent than either. The Canadians were less strongly committed to *individual* achievement and work than either; they expected more reciprocity in favours and rewards; their tendency to associate morality with religion was slightly stronger than either; they believed more strongly in private property than the English, but less strongly than the Americans; and they were more likely than Americans and Englishmen to perceive their society as given to nepotism. It also showed that, though the Canadians' commitment to democracy was not as strong as that of either the English or the Americans, they were much more skeptical of government and government officials, less committed to voluntary and civic work than either. The Canadian labour force was rated equally with the British and more than the U.S. labour force in terms of alienation. Finally, the study showed less Canadian consensus about public objectives than in either the U.S. or Britain, and notes that Canadians perceive among themselves more class structure than do the Americans, but less than the British would admit.

This study reveals a relatively clannish people, skeptical of their political institutions. Indeed, it shows Canadians to be less trusting than either the British or the Americans of 'others' in general. But here, in fact, are signs of an organic society with a comparatively strong core structure (including a substantial tendency toward nepotism). Its commitment to *individual* achievement is less than that of the other societies. But it is also a picture of an organic society under pressure. The lack of trust is matched by other doubts and fears: Canadians are less sure of personal security than the British, though a good deal more sure than Americans.

It is this rather pressed, but still alive — and lively — community which poses our problem. Let us, then, look at the idea of community in order to get closer to the idea of Canada.

Chapter 2

The Idea of Community and Our Divided Culture

A community shows itself in the institutions it legitimizes — or tries to legitimize. The structure of a community is the shape of public authority and the pattern of men's interactions with each other.

Public authority is not only a show of force. The criminal law, for instance, is effective at best against recalcitrant minorities. If even ten percent of us decided to take up bank robbing, or refused to return our library books or decided to paint slogans on the wall of the neighbourhood United Church, the authorities would probably have to give in. You can't put two million people in jail. You can't even shoot them and have much chance of surviving the resultant mess. The law works because, by and large, people accept it. It works, more exactly, because the community is coherent enough and willing enough to legitimize the legal institutions — or at least to make them seem legitimate.

The distinctions are important. It is the *institution* which is regarded as legitimate. Hardly anyone accepts the claim of every law to be legitimate. Most people, however, accept the institution and, having accepted the institution of law, accede to its demands even when they have doubts about specific laws.

It is always the institution which validates the process. A judge is just a man on the street apart from the fact that the legal institutions recognize him as a judge. So it is with our political institutions. A statute is not the law just because the prime minister and his friends consent to it. It is the law because Parliament consents to it, the Governor General gives his assent and the courts are obliged to interpret it. The system works because even those who detest the current regime for the most part accept the institution. Again, if even a fairly large minority of us chose to ignore Parliament, the system certainly would not work. We can at least imagine a country in which the legal institutions go on working — the courts continue to recognize all the old laws — but, simply, no one accepts any new ones.

For a community to remain alive and coherent, it generally must recognize and give effective shape to a range of institutions — legal, political, economic, educational, religious. Failure to do so results in a very obvious kind of crisis in which groups and individuals exercise political and legal functions arbitrarily. If the process goes too far, widespread breakdowns of the social and economic process rapidly set in.

After such revolutionary upsets, there is a tendency to bring order by arranging the institutions in a hierarchy in which one institution — usually political or religious — has control of the others. Without the jostling of institutions, with the opportunities which that brings for change and community expression, the community may then find itself cut off and impotent.

Communities may also become ineffective, obviously, if the institutions fail to work together. This failure to cohere may come about in at least two different ways. First, the functions of the institutions may be conceived in such a way that they cannot work together without friction. In the United States, for example, there is a widespread assumption that the economic institutions are intended to enrich individual participants, while it is supposed to be the function of the political institutions to safeguard the public good. Unless some 'invisible hand' reconciles what seems to be irreconcileable, clashes are inevitable. But there is always a community sentiment for a 'new deal' which it is hoped will bring about a final reconciliation. When Roosevelt replaced Hoover, there was a real sense of a resurgent community.

The second possibility is that the community may seek to legitimize too many institutions on the same level without providing an adequate order for them. Sometimes order is provided in a natural way: there are 50 states, but even the largest of them — New York and California — seem trivial compared to the United States as a whole. It takes a large regional coalition (like the South in the Civil War) to provide anything which appears to compete in crude importance. Reinforced concrete, the split-level suburb, and the super-highway have helped Burger King and Howard Johnson to reduce that country to a sameness in which state government is mainly of concern to those who want road contracts or larger appropriations for their local college.

More importantly, American institutions are American. Regionalism persists, state politicians have a great measure of independence, some causes that are overwhelmingly popular in Alabama are anathema in Oregon. But, still, a State Capitol, more often than not, is a condensed replica of the national Capitol. The two have the same inner workings, and politicians are enmeshed in a network of affiliations and deals which give even the smallest state politician an interest in what goes on in Washington.

In Canada the multiplicity of institutions creates a different effect. It is arguable, if you live in Trois Rivières, that Quebec is more important than Canada. Ontario is so large (and historically if not currently) so powerful that it has always been conceived as having an interest of its own, an interest about which fathers in British Columbia find it necessary to warn their growing children. All this is there on the surface for everyone to see. But our tendency to authorize conflicting institutions goes a good deal deeper than the mere creation of provincial legislatures. And our own crisis of community cannot be grasped if we do not dig a little deeper. Essentially, our problem has to do with the way in which the community is associated with a central culture and variety of sub-cultures.

Communities show themselves in their institutions, but they have their bases in culture. 'Culture' is a slippery word. It is used by anthropologists to describe patterns of behaviour which link together the whole lives of members of identifiable groups of people. It is often used by professors of English and teachers of the violin to evaluate certain 'civilizing' attainments, like poetry or symphonic music. It was used by T.S. Eliot in this way as the name for what he believed was good for us. Philosophers like to distinguish between these 'descriptive' and 'evaluative' uses of the term. But in fact there is a link between them.

On either the descriptive or the evaluative use of the term, culture has to do with meanings. It is not the physical movements of people's bodies which constitute the 'cultures' of which the anthropologists speak. It is the meaning that is assigned to them. It is because some behaviours are understood as religious rituals while others are understood as giving the raspberry to the umpire that we can identify and distinguish the cultures of the Upper Volta, or the Bronx, or East St Catherine's Street. But meanings are understood as parts of human intentions and thus, ultimately, as associated with the ways in which people orient their lives. In turn these orientations are expressed through — and become intelligible through — literature and art. Indeed, it is through a common sentiment articulated through painting, poetry, literature, and music that it becomes possible to *have* a culture despite all the complexities of a modern society.

To have a culture in the midst of all the pressures of this modern world is to have an understanding of meanings that can move men

The Royal Winnipeg Ballet
Arnold Spohr, Director
Featuring
Norbert Vesak's
New Ballet with
Chief Dan George

The Ecstasy of Rita Joe

Commissioned by the
Manitoba Indian
Brotherhood

From the play by George Ryga / Music: Ann Mortifee / Film: Don S. Williams

Royal Winnipeg Ballet & Public Archives of Canada (C107529)   1973

Art seeks the universal, but it gets its reality from an anchor in the particulars of place and time. Classical ballet and Chief Dan George make a neat illustration of the tension between them.

in spite of their differences. Matthew Arnold understood the link clearly and maintained that it was through culture, conceived as the arts, that we might hope to demolish class distinctions.

One must, however, grasp exactly what is going on. If culture is associated with the assignment of meanings, it is always at once universal and particular. A meaning can be shared by all. But it is always anchored in particulars. The arts are invariably concrete. Even a Bunyan, talking of the most general condition of man and of the prospects for the salvation or damnation of all men or of any man, could only make his point by evoking a powerful image of the Bedfordshire countryside and turning Christian into a real Englishman. Real cultures are anchored in particulars. A Smetana or a Dvorak can move all men, but they do so by evoking their own commitments to Czech culture. Shakespeare was unmistakably an Englishman with all the hopes and fears and most of the prejudices of his kind.

Words which make up literature have their natural habitats, technical pursuits apart, in the homely and particular affairs of individual men. We can get no more abstract than lines and patches of colour or patterns of sound which imitate no sequence found in nature. Yet even coloured patches define a space which cannot fail to be in many ways like ordinary space and is itself concrete and particular. Colours have indefinitely many associations with our ordinary habits and responses. The rhythms even of 'pure music' follow the march of ordinary or contrived events. Sequences of sound cannot help but evoke particular natural orders.

In order to make an effective universal appeal, in order to sustain a culture in Matthew Arnold's sense — the sense in which culture is what draws men together so that they may share a common meaning and reveal common values — the particular concrete social order must be strong enough to sustain a widely shared experience. The artist and the poet must draw upon more than the picayune oddities of their own affairs. If they cannot do so, they may still, of course, create art, even great art. But it will not broaden and strengthen the culture in this sense. It will be intelligible only to individuals who are already nourished well enough by the culture so as to be able to grasp idiosyncratic perspectives on it. But the common culture must exist first. Smetana could not have evoked a disembodied world sentiment. But he could not have plumbed only the depths of his own spirit either unless, of course, he had done so in a world in which someone else had already made the Czech spirit intelligible. Only then could he have supposed the context in which his private affairs would have meaning.

Bunyan's power to fascinate even those who abominate his religion derives from his ability to use an experience both wide and concrete. He could draw on the world of other Englishmen of his own time and upon the whole tradition of western culture, but he needed to bring them to earth in the town of Bedford and the person of Christian.

We can now begin to look at the situation in Canada. One cannot fail to have 'a culture.' But it may be ineffective. There is always some pattern according to which men give meaning to at least crucial clusters of behaviour. But the pattern can easily lose its coherence. Amongst the Indians of the Coast of British Columbia, for instance, the potlatch was used to validate transactions central to the functioning of the most basic institutions. Crucial changes in rank and power and the settlement of important disputes were related to a validation process in which the ceremonial giving of gifts — and at times the destruction of symbolically important property — played an indispensable part. When this ceremonial giving, potlatching, was outlawed, life still had to go on. But without the marks of validity, actions lost their crucial dimension of meaning. The fragility of the culture became apparent in a situation in which the participants had already begun to recognize, even if reluctantly, the validity of competing institutions.

This is a dramatic case but, in a way, it is typical of the whole crisis of community in Canada. At every point in our history, we have had conflicts of institutional recognition. And they have been characteristically marked by circumstances which have interfered with the validation of our institutions. We have few political heroes. Perhaps our most competent prime minister (in all the technical senses) was Mackenzie King. His name brings a smile. Whole forests have perished in the attempt to show that his grandfather, William Lyon Mackenzie, a genuinely brave (though not foolhardy) man, who shares with Papineau the rightful claim to have created the circumstances in which Canada became a politicial necessity, was not a hero but a self-serving crank. Our first prime minister, Sir John A. Macdonald, was astute and we owe him much, but his name conjures up pictures of a drunk up to his ears in railway scandals. Laurier had the makings of a real hero but the public nicknamed him "the silver fox." We have always found it hard to take our politicians seriously.

A very likely reason for this circumstance is that our political institutions were borrowed from British and American societies which had undergone quite different transformations. Our society remained committed to tightly knit communities of the kind which I have called organic, but these groups had been dispersed. The French culture in 1867 had spread west so that language groups did not form a homogenous unit. In parts of Ontario, Protestant and Catholic villages alternated along the roads through the newly opened bush. Yet we adopted the Anglo-American plan of representation by place — a notion which supposed that men and women in the same geographical region formed a representable unity. One result was that, with no way of uniting the voices of French speakers outside Quebec, Francophones in the west were outnumbered, out-pressured, and eventually simply outvoted.

The readiness to regard British and American institutions as having a natural validity has therefore tended to prevent us from creating our own. At the same time that readiness did not succeed in attaching us to those institutions with the certainty exhibited by Americans to their institutions. The Haida and the Kwakiutl lost their power to validate their own institutions and are now struggling to regain it. Canadians of European descent tended to accept the validity of conflicting institutions and had yet to develop their own means of institutional validation.

The outlawed potlatch was enshrined in myth — it was a central part of a series of artistic structures through which the coast Indians understood their relations to each other and to nature. Validation is a feature of a human world in which one feels at home, content. It starts with the transformation of nature in art — the telling of stories and the creation of objects in wood or stone or metal which are capable of preserving meaning. The Indian stories gave meaning to the landscape — the rocks and islets and harbours had places in the stories which they told. A person thus always felt at home. At the same time people and gods in the stories behaved in ways which evoked the patterns of approval and disapproval which stabilized the community.

The two senses of culture thus merge in a quest like that of Matthew Arnold for a social unity. We have lost much of our native culture, but we have created in Canada the base of an understanding which has been capable of sustaining a broad range of meanings in a way which has produced a substantial poetry, a fiction as good as any, painting of many genres and, indeed, more music than seems to have been recognized.

But this culture faces serious difficulties. The Canadian who goes to England is usually surprised to find (especially if he is an English-speaking Canadian who reads much) that everything seems familiar. The land has long since been humanized. Poems and stories which are part of nearly everyone's life have created a common experience so that not only is it true that, in a sense, one has 'been there before,' but it is also true that the landscapes have a rich variety of meaning, much of which is not conscious but which surely contributes to one's sense of feeling at home. Public institutions are familiar for the same reasons.

In Canada, by contrast, there are simple problems of time and space. The humanization of the land is, itself, a task of incredible proportions. There is an England stitched together in imaginative experience from Fielding to Forster which gradually comes to seem a unity seen from a myriad of perspectives. Arnold Bennett may have written about the potteries of the north Midlands, but his characters are as recognizably English as the spies from good public schools who populate the writings of Graham Greene. The regional novels of J.B. Priestley are part of a unified literary landscape whose country no one mistakes.

It has seemed much less so in Canada. The novels of Mordecai Richler, for instance, portray an Americanized Jewish culture juxtaposed against a bizarre portrayal of fragments of Anglo-French Montreal. The result is highly amusing and sometimes moving. It creates the sense of bewilderment of men and women trying to sustain some semblance of human balance in a mad world. But as a *Canadian* social space, it ends abruptly. It makes easy contact with the American and British cultures to which it is directed, but it meets no other Canadian space. Since its validity depends upon its ability to make contact with Americans and Englishmen (amongst whom Richler is currently perhaps our most celebrated novelist) it creates little which will validate our own culture.

Serious attempts to provide the base for a Canadian culture do not have an easy time of it. When they have caught the public imagination, the effect has sometimes been disastrous because they appear out of context to an imagination with our preoccupations. The title of Hugh McLennan's *Two Solitudes* has passed into the language as a standard expression for our predicament. The novel does, indeed, create the sense that behind its surface portrayals of Francophone and Anglophone culture in Montreal there is a continuous world which extends eastward and westward through space and far back into time. But there are too many gaps in our literary space and we have yet to have a portrayal which can embed in popular thought and culture an equally powerful image of the common features of two peoples who drink the same beer, curse the same hockey referees and could jointly understand John Diefenbaker. Marian Engel's *The Glassy Sea* recreates small town, middle class Protestantism and the effects of the transformation of its inhabitants into urbanized professionals with an eye for detail which rings true from Sarnia to New Westminster. The structure of the novel clearly implies adjoining regions whose existence explains central parts of the story. But many of these surrounding spaces remain unexplored.

It is not that the unifying features are not there if one begins to study the underlying structure of the literature — only that, for various reasons, not enough of that pattern has passed into public experience to transform that experience into a coherent whole. Robin Mathews has pointed out, for example, that the vision created by one of our most popular writers, Margaret Atwood, in *Survival*, may not only breed an unwarranted despair; but, also cause us to ignore rather a lot of important Canadian literature. The background ideas in *Survival* are tied to that of the 'garrison' mentality which stems from the thought of Northrop Frye. This in turn stems from the notion that Canada got started at the peak of the influence of a certain reading of the philosophy of René Descartes. On this reading, all experience seemed to be essentially private. I have my experience and you have yours. My joys and my pains are my own. You do not feel them. We do not, on that view, live *at all* in a world of shared experience but in a world in which each of us must infer the existence of the others. Added to this essential loneliness (the root of much subjectivism in art, poetry, and prose) was the literal isolation of man in a hostile environment.

Despite the prevalence of this interpretation, it does not really follow from Descartes' philosophy, which held that some ideas, like human reason and the ability to prove the existence of God, were common to all men. There was therefore always an effort to combat this "Cartesianism" and nowhere was this effort more consistent than in Canada. Canadian philosophers perceived nature not as hostile but as fragile and to be treated with respect. Nature was neither that plastic creature of the American sunshine to be done with as one pleases nor the virginal beauty of the European Romantics. It was there. It responded. It demanded respect. It could never be conquered, but neither could it conquer. Hence the Cartesian mentality tends to be in our thought as something itself to be resisted, and the picture is rather more complicated — as Professor Mathews insists — than Margaret Atwood recognizes.

The reasons why our own background has not emerged fully into the Canadian consciousness include the sheer magnitude of the country, our internal cultural plurality and the pull of external cultures. It will take more than a powerful literature to fuse these into a vision which is capable of validating institutions while maintaining the very pluralist virtues that are surely an important element of our reality.

Without that pluralism Canadians would mostly feel trapped and hunted, just as they feel bewildered without a vision which can fit the pieces together. The rest of us are not quite in the situation of the Haida and the Kwakiutl for whom the transformation of nature into validating myth might, as a historical matter, be looked on as a single process. Our institutions are much more impersonal — having, themselves, the character of natural objects. They need to be described and then to be given a place in art. The sheer complexity of our institutions is as yet imperfectly mediated by bonds of culture. Not only fiction is at issue.

In England or the United States, for instance, there is a literature which describes, analyzes and philosophizes about the law in thousands of volumes not just from the lawyer's point of view but from the perspectives of all the participants. Our legal literature — though very efficient on its own ground — is chiefly professional, and when it exposes broader ground it tends to be ignored or even to be regarded with hostility. In England or the United States this body of secondary literature opens the institution to art as well as knowledge. An English writer can set a scene in an English court with confidence. The English courtroom is familiar to millions who have never been in it. Canadian newspapers, themselves imitations of their American counterparts, seem to struggle to create the impression that our courts are as American as those in Chicago. Canadians called to jury duty are often surprised to find that they are not in a Perry Mason story, that crown attorneys are not district attorneys hell-bent on conviction, or that a criminal court in Saskatoon exudes an aura of worried friendliness and only rarely exhibits the high drama of personal confrontation. Part of the problem, certainly, is that we have too many different institutions and that they are too complex. But more of it is that the peculiarities of our institutions seem, by contrast, unimportant. We want to believe that Perry Mason would be quite at home in Saskatoon.

Our fascination with American culture is not specifically the work of those plotting for a kind of world cultural domination. It largely results from the fact that most of us accept the institutions of that culture as valid. This in turn has its causes in English Canada in the fact that we are comfortable in a world which has been humanized by English literature in general.

Our belief in this validity is reinforced by television, the movies and the press. The fact is, however, that up to now television and the movies have not tended to initiate the artistic forms and models which validate cultures. They imitate and disseminate. Perhaps they are too ephemeral in their effects to reformulate the bases of culture, or perhaps we have not yet learned to use them effectively. But though they do reinforce our outlooks and habits, our taste for American television is surely predicated on the fact that we already accept American culture. To shut it off would not quite be like trying to cure the measles by covering up the spots, for it would at least slow down the addictive process. But if there should be or could be a cure, it *would* depend on a willingness to turn it off.

The problem is different but not necessarily less pressing in French Canada. French-Canadians do not automatically accept French institutions as valid though, as the power of the church has waned, French institutions have probably become more attractive to some. Quebecers have not modelled their universities on those of France (but are they not also becoming rather American?) Their church has been their own. Their economic institutions are often identical with those of English Canada, and when they are not, they are more American than French. They have struggled as English-Canadians have to make alien political institutions their own. They have recently been clearly more determined than English-Canadians to find ways of validating their own institutions. They do not start from an empty social space, but from a rich history. The question, as for English-Canadians, concerns how one situates oneself in that history.

Jean Charbonneau, philosopher, poet, playwright and sophisticated man of letters, seized on the idea (also briefly hinted at by François-Xavier Garneau) that French Canada is really the natural continuation of the civilization which has its beginnings in the Roman Empire. That Empire he saw transformed by Christianity and gradually moulded into a community of mutual responsibility — a community elsewhere sundered by the individualism of the enlightenment and by what he saw as decadence in French thought in the later part of the nineteenth century. In Quebec, a sounder society endured.

Charbonneau himself tended to be a Stoic and a pantheist, and he saw the dominance of the Church in Quebec as only a phase in that development (and was therefore frequently attacked by the Church). In this way, he could explain how Canadians might appropriate the traditional conditions of validity and make them their own, though he did not, I think, expect English-Canadians to join with enthusiasm in this idea.

If we accept other institutions as valid, we must find out what their conditions of validity are. Validity always comes from some tradition. Charbonneau's notions pose a challenge: one cannot simply overthrow a tradition. One always seeks to transform it in the name of some of the values which it instantiates. Even a revolutionary like Marx was pitting certain values from that tradition which goes back to Greece and Rome against other values embedded in the same tradition — humanity, justice and equality against security of possession. In taking a long view, Charbonneau tries to distinguish the accidental features which figure only in certain phases of the tradition from the essential. It was the toughness with which, he thought, a handful of Frenchmen had built a civilization in Quebec against a background of neglect, hostility, and even apparent defeat, which, in Charbonneau's view, revealed the reality of that historical continuity.

A theory of history is thus essential — Marx insisted on it as much as Charbonneau. In Quebec, the swirl of modern cultures and the divorce of education from the classics and from a classical outlook on the world severely limited the efficacy of such notions as Charbonneau's. But they continue to pose a challenge.

Neither English-Canadians nor the Haida Indians can so easily latch onto the Roman Empire. The English-Canadian heritage goes back into the clashes of the Romans and the barbarians, and in imagination we may well see ourselves on the other side. A past generation tried valiantly to integrate us into the historical web of the British Empire, but the problem was not so much that they failed to be persuasive as that the Empire proved to be short-lived. Others have seen us as merely a deviant offshoot of the American branch of the thrust toward enlightenment individualism.

It might not matter so much that English-Canadians tended to be enmeshed in conflicting parts of the Anglo-American culture if, in fact, they could be happy at it. (Though it *would* matter, for we would have lost one of the possibilities of being human if we lost our own culture.) But they are no more at home in that conflict than the French-Canadians. All we know about ourselves shows a people with an outlook of its own, significantly alienated from the institutions validated by other cultures. Attempts to imitate those cultures are not only unsatisfying, they tend to be gloomily second-rate. Our imitations of American television programmes, magazines and newspapers are no better than American imitations of our nurse fiction, the only literary genre in which, if one may judge from a look at the news-stands, we currently dominate the continent.

Given that we cannot so easily accept assimilation, we must look more closely at the underpinnings of our situation. It seems obvious that the problem is not with the internal workings and quality of the culture, but with its context. To be sure, it needs some support and stimulation but there is a good working base already there. The problem is not even with the plurality. Perhaps many of the same cultural traits of a Scots highlander and a French peasant can be more easily shared with a Haida Indian than can the traits of a Bronx stockbroker or a London barrow boy. We must then look at some of the other forces at work in the world.

Chapter 3

Technology, Economics and the Transformation of Space and Time

C ulture in Canada in many ways is healthy and exciting. But it has not yet fully gripped the conscious imagination. Northrop Frye has remarked — somewhat wryly — that our regionalism may even be a sign of maturity. The irony comes out if one looks at the whole of what he says:

> Regionalism is an inevitable part of the maturing of a culture like ours. I think that in this 'instant world of communications,' as it is called, there is a kind of uniform international way of seeing and thinking which is derived from the fact that everybody is involved in the same technology. Regional developments are a way of escaping from that, developing something more creative.

Frye holds that cultural fragmentation may be a response — even an intelligent one — to the unification imposed by technology. Indeed, cultural fragmentation appears to be of surprisingly little importance in economic institutions whether in Canada or anywhere else in the modern world. It is not merely that products are universal — Pepsi-Cola is in demand in Russia, Coca-Cola sells in China, Soviet cars are built in cooperation with Fiat, cheques are signed in Paris with Parker pens, Hoovers hustle dirt for people who address them in nearly every language.

It is the technique of mass production which is universal, and everywhere its demands are the same: to have mass production one must have mass consumption; to have mass consumption one must create a common pattern of demand. And one must organize human activity so that those who work do so in an orderly way and those who consume do so according to the pattern which best fits the productive capacity.

The first puzzle one faces in thinking about it is to explain how it is that this unification can possibly accompany cultural fragmentation. Indeed, the very fact that this unifying process is at work everywhere has raised the thought that the talk about culture and frágmentation may just be so much intellectualized noise —dreams and nightmares produced by those who live snugly in the academy and fail to notice that in the outside world people are really concerned with new cars, dishwashers, football games and soap operas.

There is a kind of pretense morality and mock seriousness which lies behind the thesis that serving the public interest just consists in providing those objects which pander to the imagined popular taste. That this is not very serious — or is at least puzzling to those who hold it — is shown by the fact that even in the centre of the culture from which such things most often come, few young men just out of the Harvard Business School actually itch to control a company which makes coloured condoms, or to wrest control of the East Texas Plastic Jesus Company from whatever captain of industry now runs it. One is usually expected to make a case for the proposition that one is filling a 'real' need — for, if nothing else, there is a suspicion that 'real' need (as opposed to manufactured 'need,' like the 'need' for whatever latest fad may be created by a television commercial) is linked to steady, long-range demand.

But there is something more than a little strange beneath this placid picture of honest widget makers sitting earnestly around their boardroom tables wondering how they can make life better for housewives in Sioux Falls, South Dakota. No one knows just why or how it is that the deodorant business produces a product which has become a permanent necessity, while the yo-yo industry has its ups and downs and the pressure cooker has become rarer than the United Church hymn book. Nor, indeed, does anyone know what a 'real need' is, except that responding to it is what all good citizens must do in order to keep the company going.

And, while most of us respond well enough to the televised call to make life better for our fellows by using suitable deodorants, we eventually respond sluggishly to new demands in a world in which our duty to consume is always one step beyond our means, and in which the things we consume must necessarily give no more than momentary satisfaction. We must thus be constantly stimulated by ever more costly advertising campaigns and convinced that it is positively immoral to be satisfied; for one who is satisfied responds to no new calls to consume, and will soon learn from the TV screen that he is a pariah who will be shunned by all those who made themselves more lovable by acquiring the new necessities.

We may not all react to our inability to do our economic duty as the prosperous Swedes are rumoured to react by committing suicide. Some of us go away and read a book. But there is a grim reality behind all this which makes the concern about culture more than a passing whim.

In the background, for instance, are growing lines of people, the kinds of people who used to be in a mental hospital, but who now wait patiently for their tranquilizers. In the twenty years after 1955, annual admissions to mental hospitals in the United States doubled (from 178,003 in 1955 to 374,654 in 1974), though the population which remained *in* the hospitals declined by more than half, from 558,992 in 1955 to 215,573 in 1974. In Canada, the population in mental hospitals continued to fall as well, though 35,000 per year (just about the same rate as in the United States) were being admitted. These are only the most serious cases. It is difficult to say what number of people are taking tranquilizers every day, but it has undoubtedly grown quite steadily for a quarter of a century.

These stressful people are at the *head* of the queue of those for whom the industrializing process has created a world in which one must look inward for satisfaction and for whom that inward view is apt to seem empty. It is useful again to look at the case in the heartland of 'international' culture: historically, one thinks of Americans as confident in their institutions; indeed, characteristic complaints about life in the United States have always taken the form of assertions that whatever it is that oppresses one is inconsistent with the whole American way of life. Yet a recent Harris Poll reveals an astonishing collapse of Americans' expressed public trust in a variety of institutions. The percentage of respondents who expressed "a great deal of confidence" in the leadership of various institutions fell in many cases by half or more in the decade and a half from 1966 to 1979/80. In the last year only 33% had "a great deal" of confidence in the leadership of higher education, 30% in medicine, 20% in organized religion, 19% in major companies, 33% in the military. These responses had fallen from 61% in higher education, 73% in medicine, 41% in organized religion, 55% in major companies and 61% in the military. The press had fallen only 7%, but it had started with a dismal 27%. Only confidence in the White House fell not at all. The sturdy 18% who were confident in it in 1966 remained so a decade and a half later. Data like this and much else besides had led David Reissman, the established U.S. sociologist-hero of the 1950s, to the dismal conclusion in 1980 that the American character is changing, that ego-centrism is on the march, and that the social bonds are creaking.

In fact, though modern technology perforce unites behaviour in

CPR Archives (14413)   M. Leone Bracker, 1931

A dream and a reality: The great CPR locomotives were amongst Canada's triumphs. Here the machine looms a little ominously, though. The machine triumphed over individuality. Does one dream of today's diesel locomotives as well?

the literal sense that it compels hundreds of millions of men in many different parts of the world to go through the same motions, it also tends to deprive these same actions of many dimensions of meaning. It thus compels a search for meaning which is very likely in capitalist society to be turned inward. But inward visions are notoriously subjective and this is surely, itself, one of the sources of the fragmentation of culture and thus of the crisis of community. I am not sure that this is maturity.

A mediaeval man faced an outer world which could, with the materials at hand, readily be given a meaning in terms of a world vision centred on the struggle for salvation and damnation. Almost any man-made object he came into contact with in daily life could be made to symbolize a feature of this world, and his picture of the natural world enabled him to think of natural objects as functioning just as directly in some divine plan. Even so, social tensions existed and culture was far from homogenous. The agricultural and industrial techniques of the time, combined with the available means of passing messages and organizing people, limited the available wealth and made periodic shortages fairly common-place. They also combined to produce a situation in which political power was concentrated in relatively small pockets centred on large towns and trade routes. It was necessary to have an organization, therefore, to deal with intruders, threats to trade, the problems created by occasional famines and so forth. Local stability was provided in some measure by passing on wealth and certain offices to one's immediate heirs, thereby slightly reducing the likelihood of power struggles.

A society whose official ideology had a marked 'other-worldly' outlook had also to sustain a substantial class of persons dedicated to religion whose authority was a natural outcome of their relation to the claims to special knowledge which the ideology authorized, but who usually were well placed to withstand whatever strains the system produced. In such a world a man could, for the most part, find meaning in his daily task and a significance for his life in a scheme of cosmic proportions. He lived in a community which shared the same general view and within which, in turn, he had a precise place. It might be difficult for him to move from it, but it was also difficult to move it from him.

By and large the ideology was powerful enough to keep the difficulties within bounds, and the thirteenth century saw one of the great burgeonings of human civilization. Its breakdown was heralded by a more individualistic ideology accompanied by plague, famine, rapid technological change, and the creation of circumstances which were increasingly depersonalized. The disarray of plagues and famines combined with improving technologies (the crossbow, better ships, clearer ideas of navigation) opened up the possibilities for political organizations which spread farther and organized more deeply, gradually creating units of political allegiance more distant from the individual, as well as regions through which individuals could move with more freedom.

The space relevant to political activity thus changed its nature. It was becoming more abstract — one had to think of France, not of one's village or one's region. It was becoming less clearly structured. New organizations could (and eventually did) produce not only new social functions but whole new social classes. The tie of wealth to land was loosened and the relative importance of traders and landowners shifted from generation to generation.

Cities could be and were humanized. Ships can take on magical properties as well as cathedrals, new social functions can become as cosy as the old ones. But the possibilities for human organization grew. The beginnings of the factory were certainly present in the water-driven industries of the middle ages. But as such organizations grew, the separation of the individual from his product became inevitable. So, too, did the integration of production into the world of objects which could not so easily be transformed into an environment which had meaning beyond itself. The control of large spaces over long spans of time requires nuts, bolts, iron girders, concrete blocks — all the apparatus of modern industry, vast numbers of industrial items which can be made to match precise standards and which will be interchangeable everywhere. Such items, in being standardized, become depersonalized. The one surely implies the other.

Such a system can produce, of course, as it finally did, things which will take much of the drudgery out of life — vacuum cleaners and dishwashers as well as pneumatic drills and backhoes to dig ditches. But it is important to realize that a world populated with such devices will be a world in which the ideology of the middle ages, for example, will be quite hard to sustain. The mediaeval ideology depended upon a world in which nearly every event and object in life could be seen to have a religious as well as secular significance. But one cannot have toasters in the form of a crucifix; no art can transform a vacuum cleaner into an object which points to a transcendent world.

The creation of the modern world had to bring with it the creation of at least a large number of modern men — men who could, like nuts and bolts, be interchanged with each other and who had been trained to precise and high standards, much as good tools are machined. The industrial world will work only if, for instance, nearly all mechanical engineers react in the same way to the same situation. One is not to stand looking dreamily at the printing press and thinking about eternity; one must now think of one's capital investment, of the balance sheet, of the activities of one's competitors. Failure to act in the required way will result in one's being replaced by another technician with exactly the same skills but a clearer understanding of what is expected of him.

Indeed, it was the creation of standard men — men trained for specific pre-determined tasks and trained in adequate numbers to provide at least a slight surplus — that led to the situation which now confronts us most brutally: men in competition. The banker forecloses on the mortgage holder not because he wants to or because he is greedy (he almost certainly has nothing personal to gain) but because, if he doesn't, a more efficient banker will have his job to-morrow. If a whole bank should go soft, it would, of course, be replaced by a more competitive bank.

Curiously enough, this process itself has also re-oriented time. Harold Innis remarked that one of the clues to the historical understanding of any era is something which we often fail to notice: a grasp of the concept of time in use or in vogue, and the way in which it is associated with the knowledge characteristic of the period. The process of the creation of standard men for standard tasks and the resultant competition did more than anything else to orient time from a dominantly (but not wholly) cyclical notion to a linear notion which has plagued us ever since. Traditionally, time ran in cycles. One measured the year from harvest to harvest. One patterned each day in cycles like its predecessors. Human life itself formed a natural cycle. It was not meant to go anywhere but to complete its natural task.

A competitive world, however, is one in which each man has to add something and keep adding something or be replaced. Each sales manager must sell more than his predecessor. Each factory must make more (more product, more money) this year than last. The world goes forward like the stock-market graph in the *Globe and Mail* — a square a day. No one knows where it is headed or why. Our image of time is of a line stretching from the distant past into the endless future, just like the graph. The disorienting features of this scheme are enormous. At the very least, in such a picture, each of us sees himself trivialized from the perspective of the future — a mere speck in a distant past. As time goes on, in many realms, 'adding something' becomes harder if not impossible.

But the real difficulty is that the scheme finally breaks down. In its infancy, the doctrine of Progress seemed natural enough. Things must get bigger, better, richer. For technology adds something in each generation, as each man adds something to what his predecessor achieved. Knowledge itself comes to be seen in terms of this model. Each inquirer must add something. Originality is all. Yesterday's knowledge is outdated. Plotinus pales into insignificance compared to Willard Quine, Harvard's principal logician of the day.

It has gradually emerged that we are not necessarily going anywhere. Progress turned out to have many meanings. The First World War produced poison gas; the Second World War the flame thrower, the fire bomb and the atomic bomb. By the Vietnam War it was common practice for U.S. soldiers to burn children alive with jellied gasoline and then to add a chemical which made them burn even more brightly if they tried to put out the flames with water.

There seems, as the study of public opinion in the United States showed, to be a crisis of nerve, a loss of confidence in the whole system. But there is also a massive disorganization created, at least in part, by the fact that people eventually react sluggishly to a never-ending set of meaningless demands for change and expansion, and require ever more stimulation. Our ways of stimulating people have not become very much more effective than they were a generation ago; but, as endless stimulation wears thin, it may be that too many simply become numbed and lose interest —especially in a long-range future seen as an endless set of meaningless events.

Nostalgia is a common phenomenon in all the 'western democracies' — leaving Ronald Reagan, a man who seems to belong to the world of a generation ago, walking the stage in the United States, and holding hands across the sea with his British counterpart, Maggie Thatcher. Duplessis is suddenly remembered with affection by some in Quebec, and even Mussolini seems to be recovering a certain following in Italy. That may be a very temporary response, but it will likely be replaced by an equally irrational one, unless there is some massive change in the system.

To find the causes of this failure of nerve we shall have to dig rather deep, and to overcome it we shall have to make some quite basic changes. In Canada, as in any country some distance from the centre of the world technology and economy, the problems are compounded. When a crisis comes, it is not the factory in the United States that is closed, but the branch plant in Canada. It is not the peculiarities of Canadian life and environment that one serves, but the common pattern. Research and development are, naturally, done as close as possible to the point at which the planning is done. And, above all, the factory in Canada is not to set itself up in competition with the U.S. home office for the conquest of foreign markets. Thus, though there is little unique in our confrontation with technology and the modern world economy, we are forced to think harder about it than the Germans or the Japanese.

One can see, however, just how it is that important elements in the culture come to float free from the economic system and how, therefore, that culture may fragment all too easily: as the outside world becomes increasingly empty and meaningless, meanings tend to become internalized. It is this meaninglessness which allows the economic system to rampage about like a dazed hippopotamus, surfacing to strike whom it may. Culture, as the pattern of meanings, becomes increasingly unstructured. Art, literature, and music are apt to become amusements which do little more than distract because they are not closely tied to any external reality. They themselves may also become progressively empty.

An internalized culture also fragments very easily — there is nothing to hold it. The best one can do with it is to turn it into an industry and harness it in the sale of deodorants. But even that becomes less and less effective. We have had, in Canada, rather a good time of late exploring our inner lives. But we do not have many poets who celebrate our public life, or novelists who find deep meaning in our political life. We shall have to look not internally but 'out there' for a theory to understand, and a method to resolve, our crisis of community.

Part II

Looking for a Theory

Chapter 4

History, Community and Knowledge: the Search for a Base

*T*he most influential attempts to track down the deeper reasons for the crisis of our time — those of Hegel, Marx and Freud — all attack some aspect or other of a certain very general but violently destructive view of human nature, values, and society: the view that values are individual, that man is a mechanism for producing pleasure, and that society exists merely to reconcile conflicting desires.

It seems odd to call this view violently destructive, even if it is the world view which ushered in the American Revolution and the French Revolution. Who is against liberty, fraternity, and equality? The same view of the world sustained Jeremy Bentham in his search for "the greatest happiness of the greatest number" and John Stuart Mill in his campaign against Victorian stuffiness.

But Hegel, Marx and Freud all believed that it was facile, dangerous and destructive to suppose that we can simply remake the world as we please, that we can pander to "the pleasure principle" without paying a price, that each and every human being can be free without sharing in the lives of the others. The message was hardly new. The view that man can simply reconstitute the world at whim, and that the purpose of life is to maximize pleasure, had been denounced by the British Neo-Platonists who were in on the birth of capitalism (remember John Donne's "no man is an island"?) In philosophy they belonged to a distinguished line which included Plato, Plotinus, Boethius, John the Scot, Duns Scotus, and Nicholas of Cusa. But the modern form of the individualist doctrine belongs to what is usually called 'the enlightenment,' and the modern attempt to get at the real roots of human bondage dates from Hegel, or perhaps from Spinoza to whom Hegel ascribed many of his own insights.

According to the mythology of the individualists and the pleasure seekers Hegel is dark and unintelligible. Of course, if one believes (as many contemporary American philosophers led by

John Rawls and Robert Nozick do) that rational behaviour *consists* in pursuing one's own interests as efficiently as possible, then Hegel is simply irrational. Hegel did have new ideas and those are always hard to express in old language. And he had to wrestle with some very difficult notions. Neither reality itself nor the man-made structures which characterized his own time proved to be simple. But the central ideas of his social diagnosis are not so very difficult, and we can look at Hegel's central ideas about man and history without even introducing any strange words. There may be a little effort involved, but it is probably worth it. Maurice Merleau-Ponty, who was to post-war academic philosophy in France what Jean-Paul Sartre was to popular philosophy, remarked that "Hegel is the source of everything great in the philosophy of the last hundred years — for instance of Marxism, of Nietzsche, of German existentialism, of phenomenology, of psychoanalysis." He added: "If we are not to renounce the hope of truth ... we (must) hold onto the promise of ... an organic civilization. In the cultural realm, there is no task more urgent than to retrace to their Hegelian origins the ungrateful doctrines which seek to forget them." Even two American logicians, Irving Copi and James A. Gould, recently remarked, "Hegel's writings are considered outdated today only in the English-speaking world."

Hegel's concerns about politics and the human condition arose directly out of the aftermath to the French Revolution. He had supported the revolution: here at last was a widespread popular uprising directed against arbitrary authority and devoted to individual integrity, the brotherhood of man, and the hope of equality. The American Revolution had drawn its support largely from merchants, manufacturers and land-owners who wanted the rights and privileges already accorded to their counterparts in England. The French Revolution, in theory at least, aimed to go further and to establish a society based on reason and dedicated to justice. But the revolution was followed quickly by the Terror, and then by Napoleon.

Symbolically, the French Revolution marked the end of the nominal control of public life in western Europe by a hereditary aristocracy. In reality, it marked the unquestioned acceptance of the power of a bourgeoisie devoted to trade and manufacture. It in effect acknowledged the principle that wealth should be distributed to the winners of certain competitions — some in the business world, others, in France above all, in the realm of state-controlled public education. In one way or another, the greater part of the population was still denied the conditions for success in those competitions. The poor were to try their luck more than once on the barricades of Paris; they were able to prove that the new technology had created a 'mass' capable of 'mass action,' but not, in Hegel's time, capable of the sustained cooperative activity which might create a new society.

Two questions concerned Hegel: why did the Revolution turn into the Terror and then to an autocracy, and why was sustained cooperative activity apparently impossible? These questions were later to be put by others in many different ways. Think ahead a hundred years to 1914: why did a seemingly prosperous Europe in which 'liberal democracy' was making daily progress suddenly dissolve into a morass of mindless violence, and why were the hundreds of thousands of men, up to their necks in French mud, cursing every minute of the war, unable to put an end to it? There are always the same *underlying* questions behind them: why do some men seek to control others, and why do the others not create an organization which makes such control impossible?

Hegel thought that one needed to go back to the roots of Western civilization for answers. In a sense, as he argued in his massive *Phenomenology of Mind*, we carry the history of our civilization with us — each of us has a structure to his consciousness which reflects the experiences through which men have painfully reached their present state of awareness. It is passed on from generation to generation in our habitual ways of thinking about things. We organize our world and our relations with each other in ways that are embedded in our habits of thought. But this structure is largely unconscious. It is as if you had been born with rose-coloured glasses built into your visual apparatus. Everything would seem rose-coloured and you would think *that* was how the world was. Without anything to contrast your vision with, you couldn't tell how things objectively were. So it is if your habitual ways of thought order your experiences for you. There are assumptions which you make but of which you cannot easily be aware.

Moreover, it was Hegel's view that this structure of consciousness was not a set of ideas in what has become the standard sense of the word 'idea' — something inside one's head. Rather this structure was reflected in all the forms of social organization. What Hegel called "objective spirit" is the order one finds in the army, in the bureaucracy, in the church — in whatever social order there is.

Some more recent philosophers have believed that these habitual ways of thought are built into language. But Hegel realized that if language were *all* that were at issue we could surely overcome the problems quite easily. Language is governed by rules but poets and philosophers are always breaking the rules. Indeed, for every rule there is another rule which is its negation, and the one always suggests the other. Mere language can be mastered and is being mastered all the time.

There *is* an 'inward' or 'mental' side to these structures of thought, but it too is, in Hegel's view, substantially influenced by the institutions of the public world. Language does reflect something of the underlying ways of thought. Organizing ideas are expressed through language but never exhausted by it. The poet can always wrench something new from it — and in so doing reveals a little more of its structure. In Hegel's view, the poet is thus the friend of knowledge and not, as Plato thought, its enemy.

Yet the underlying structures of experience tend to elude consciousness. Think for a moment of the concept of space which appears in all our ordinary perception and in all our visual arts. We are always aware of something in space — never, quite, of space *itself*. Nor is it easy to think of a world which is not in space *at all*. So it tends to be even with our political ideas. The underlying organizing ideas never quite come into consciousness, but we are hard put to think of a world without them. Hegel conceived that we might bring them, at least partly, into awareness, if we could understand the processes through which they came to be developed.

In the end, he concluded that it is the concept of freedom which lies at the bottom of political notions. But freedom is not a clearly formulated idea. What is it to be free? To be able to do what you want? To be able to do what you ought to do? To be able to want what it is reasonable to want? A man might feel *most* free if he only wanted to do what his conscience told him he ought to do, or his reason told him he could do. Hegel thought that the idea of freedom functions in political life somewhat in the way that our ideas of space function in organizing what we see. It tends to organize our other demands without itself being very clear.

But it does have a history which can be traced in western civilization to the breakdown of tribalism and the development of the despotisms of the ancient Near East. Here, we can expose just enough of history as Hegel saw it to be able to see the principle he is looking for, and to be able to grasp something of his method.

Let us imagine a society (which we can call a tribe) in which everyone has a function and lives overlap as well as intersect, so that the notion of its component members as unique individuals does not arise in the way that has become common in our societies but is always set against a context in which the community is an experienced reality. There will be large areas of shared experience, and these shared experiences will tend to control the relation of the individual to the community. Nevertheless, there will be an underlying tension. Individuals will exist. If nothing else, the simple laws of genetics will virtually guarantee that no two individuals are biologically identical. But they will exist in a world in which most activities are shared with others and most tasks are performed according to rules and standards so deeply established that their origins are known only in myth. Individual expression may be difficult to achieve. Even — perhaps especially — art is apt to be stylized and embedded in ritual. Such a society may be stable for very long periods of time, but the tension will emerge if it is subjected to external stress or internal change of an unusual kind. For though there may well be a king, a chief, or a headman, there will not be the differentiated apparatus of a state.

This is the world which Plato often seems to be recalling: one in which the king stands because of his merit — because he well exemplifies the virtues of the tribe — and not because he has the power to compel others to obey. For in such a society (as Pierre Clastres who has studied living examples has recently pointed out) the ruler really has no political power as we understand it. There is no police force and no army to do his bidding. He must rely on the response of the whole community.

The changes which led to the growth of civilization (for the moment we can take 'civilization' in its literal sense of 'becoming citified') amongst the ancient Greeks and their Oriental neighbours were numerous, but they need only have been slight. For the tribal society depends on a careful internal balance and a precise relationship with its environment. We have learned to our cost how fragile such things are. One would need only a small technological change (the introduction of workable metals, for instance) to produce new tasks which men wanted to perform for their own sakes and which therefore produced a surplus. The Greeks at any rate lived near societies with things to sell and they became interested in trade. That meant an interchange of persons amongst cultures and would have produced fairly rapid social change. The intermingling exposed a clash of values and of religions. If one grows wealthy, one is, as Plato noticed, certain to become interesting to outsiders: pirates, brigands and assorted warlords.

Protection meant power assigned to armies which could influence internal as well as external affairs and, above all, a need for decisions. The simplest way to get decisions made is to assign absolute power to someone, and it is not surprising that societies should from time to time hit upon such a notion, though it is rarely or never put in those pragmatic terms. More often, such changes are justified on the basis of religious revelation, though it would be foolish to suppose that there is some general rule about it.

The situation of the 'despot' is a kind of inversion of the tribal society. In the kind of tribal society about which we have been talking, freedom is dispersed through the community and tends to belong to the community as a whole. But it is difficult to exercise because the dispersion is made possible through a system in which tradition plays the dominant role in decision making. When the system breaks down, freedom tends still to be unified. The power of the chief may once have been non-existent or mainly ceremonial, but it can easily be transformed into the power of the 'oriental despot' of classical times.

In reality, we find societies in states of transition. The underlying structure tends to shift the society from one pole to the other. The shift creates a new tension. Once the shift has taken place, the despot alone appears to be 'free' and everyone else is in some sense his slave. He is not really 'free' since his alleged freedom depends, in fact, on the likelihood that everyone else will do his bidding. He will usually try to assure this by creating at least one privileged class of persons who will have reason to want the others to do his bidding. Gradually, the role of despot spreads. Tyranny becomes oligarchy. Those denied 'freedom' now see what it is. It is not that they 'want' freedom but that the drawing of lines creates tensions and factions so that there is, in the end, little option but to participate in a struggle for a kind of primitive democracy.

In ancient Greece, the transition from tribalism to despotism, to a kind of limited democracy (and sometimes back to despotism) was often quite rapid. Plato had noticed, however, that the 'democracy' was suspect. Everyone demands freedom *in the same sense* that the despot has freedom. It is the freedom to do what one wants independently of the others.

Such a notion, as Hegel would have it, is self-contradictory: if I can only be free by having you do what I say and you can be free only if I do what you say, we cannot both be free unless we are able to agree on what we are to do. But if we do agree, then we are bound by the agreement and we are also not (in the original sense) free. Compromise takes forms with which we are all too familiar.

Hegel regards the Greek idea of freedom as bound up with Greek art and therefore as one of the high points in history. The decline of Athens, like the fall of Rome, remains one of the great tragedies of history, and it must not be supposed that Hegel was

ilistine enough to prefer dreary German bureaucracy to the
citement of the Agora. Indeed, one must remember that he is
ying to find out where the sickness of the civilization of the west set
i. It is not a foregone conclusion that the breakup of the tribe was a
good thing, and it is not, for Hegel, at all likely that any other
history will exactly parallel ours. Furthermore, he understands
better than anyone perhaps that our great achievements have been
closely related to our great weaknesses. Nevertheless, he insists that
the system doomed itself by compelling government by faction.
Similarly, Rome was to fall, in Hegel's view, from internal causes
and its fall represented 'progress' within the confines of a system in
which the idea of freedom must work itself out. But one must not
suppose that Hegel found its fall a cause for simple-minded
rejoicing.

A Greek political 'faction' in the Athens of the time of Plato and
Aristotle tended to be an organization much like the Liberal Party
in Canada. Its aim was to stay in power. That is not to say that its
leaders did not have good deeds in mind. But they tended to be like
the bright young lights in our NDP more often than they were
like Socrates or the fatherly old men in the CCF: they supposed that
there was little point in advancing principles if one did not acquire
power to back them with. To stay in power on these terms, the
faction had to create advantages for its supporters and disadvantages for its opponents. Such opportunities are always legion. In
any system, laws which many people want to contravene have to be
enforced rather selectively. In Athens, one of the larger classes of
offences against the law consisted of assaults on olive trees which
were sacred because of their association with the goddess Athena.
Even dead ones were, in effect, 'historic monuments' and farmers
battled the inspectors over them. Inspectors of sacred olive trees,
like members of the zoning and historical monuments boards in our
time, were provided with interesting opportunities. Oratory was a
trade taught in Plato's time by 'sophists,' much as the skillful use of
television and public opinion polls is now taught by professors of
communications. Plato complained that, like our modern professors, they confused the trappings of persuasion with the instruments
of knowledge. Athenians often imported such professors from near-
by states, just as we do. A local man may have a stronger concern for
the continued well being of the community — or, as Harold Innis
once suggested, be more willing to risk himself in rocking the boat.
Such a man might prefer to teach truth rather than tactics. He
would thus exhibit the inefficiency of a Socrates. Socrates, who
was not thought highly of by the sophists, chose death rather than a

betrayal of the laws of Athens. He was widely thought to be insane. So obvious did it seem that power could only be had and maintained in devious ways that honest Greeks in 'democratic' times and places, like serious men in British Columbia, tended to stay out of politics. Systems were sometimes devised — office holding by lot, for instance — to compel them to serve. (These have not yet been tried in British Columbia.) Other groups, like the Spartans, much admired by Plato and by some Tories of our own day, clung as fiercely as they could to the old tribal ways in order to avoid the disasters of the new freedoms. Alas, the idyllic life of the tribe is not so easily recaptured, and the Spartans of our (and Plato's) imagination probably resemble more nearly an English public school than the real thing.

In the tribal society or under despotism, freedom, where it existed at all, was unified and could be exercised consistently. In the 'all against all' individualist democracy, freedom is fragmented and dispersed throughout at least some part of the society. In ancient Greece it was dispersed throughout a citizen class which depended for its continued existence on slavery and military power. Some *individuals* were, or seemed to be, free. But their freedom set them against each other.

Such a society is naturally riddled with tensions created by the system itself. The incomplete idea of freedom which it embodies demands division and dissent. One must *create* the circumstances in which a democracy based on the promotion of self-advantage can function. The process in Athens started, perhaps, with the reforms of Solon in 593 B.C. By the death of Plato in 397 B.C., Athens was already in a perilous position. In 86 B.C., the Romans, under Sulla, sacked it.

The ordinary Athenian would not have found it easy to grasp that what was wrong with his politics was the idea of freedom embodied in the system. He would have thought that the problems were the usual ones: not enough power to repel the Romans, not enough good deals with neighbouring city states, too many inspectors arguing about the sacred olive trees, too many professors corrupting the youth. And he would have thought that the ideologies which separated the factions were real responses to real problems. But the notion that everyone should be free in the way that the despot was free prevented an effective and stable political organization because it created conditions under which factionalism was certain to arise and under which no lasting political organization extending much beyond a single city state was even possible. The Greeks understood well enough that it was a paradox that a single Greek culture should be divided against itself, but most thought that, by electing a peace party or a war party — as the case might be — one could solve the problem. Yet the city states, like the individuals, could not all be free in the way that the tyrant who rules over everybody is free.

Again, according to Hegel, there was a shift toward an opposite pole. Athens was followed by Rome as the centre of the world. Primitive democracy gave way in the end to a legal system. The concrete freedom of the individual to do what he likes is to be contrasted with the abstract notion of freedom under law. And it was this abstract idea of law which, more than anything else perhaps, enabled the Romans to rule vast areas which others had failed to unite.

In Hegel's view, this shift also represented a further step in the development of the idea of freedom. Greek freedom was still, despite Plato's objections and Aristotle's attempts at compromise, the freedom of one against all. The law existed but it was still entangled with the notion of the edict of a ruler — a law which took its authority from the fact that someone in authority willed it, and which applied to whatever group of individuals the ruler chose to or had to designate. In Rome, it continued to be true that there was not one law for everybody, but by extending citizenship beyond the inhabitants of Rome and by making citizenship something which could itself be conferred according to rule, the law that developed in Rome represented the first step toward a notion of freedom under which one man's freedom is not attained at the expense of another's.

Indeed, it is Hegel's contention — often thought paradoxical —that law so conceived is not the restriction of real freedom but, ultimately, its source. The ideal of law which began to take shape in the Roman empire was the idea of a system which confers some power according to a rule which is universal and so creates freedom which is not bought at the expense of others.

For instance, my belief that I am free to walk about in downtown Ottawa depends upon my belief that no one will hit me over the head or stick a knife in me. I could achieve that assurance by acquiring Rideau Street as my private property and barricading it against all comers. But that prevents others from having the same freedom. Alternatively, we can have a universal prohibition against hitting people over the head and sticking knives in them. Then everyone can enjoy the same freedom.

Now suppose we think of freedom, for the moment, as the power to do anything which a reasonable and sane man would want to do, but not the power to do what unreasonable and insane men would want to do. Suppose, that is, we take the view that unreasonable and insane men are *not* free; they are driven by their whims, their delusions, their brain states, their endocrine glands or whatever. Ideally, on such terms, we can imagine a legal system in which all prohibitions are of this sort. Such a system would work if it were really true that what reasonable men freely want would create cooperation and not conflict. Hegel supposed that reason was ultimately of this kind.

He did not imagine, of course, that the Roman law was like this — only that the Roman law introduced the idea of universality and so opened the gates to a new notion of freedom. It also, by relying (often at least) on laws which depended on *rules* and not merely on edicts of *rulers*, began to introduce the notion that reasons should be given for legal decisions. And this is the beginning of the appearance of this larger notion of reason.

In fact, the Roman system also introduced notions of tolerance: one could do whatever was not prohibited by the rules (as opposed to whatever was not opposed by the ruling faction), and this led to the toleration of a variety of cultures, itself a major factor in the success of the Roman system of government. It was this which led the Romans into conflict first with the Jews and then with the Christians. For Jew and Christian alike refused the normal conditions of tolerance in the Roman world, which began with a recognition (if only symbolically) of one another's gods.

The ideas behind the Roman system did not emerge suddenly and were never wholly victorious. They arose out of components of Greek culture and out of the breakdown of Greek civilization. Plato had had a difficult time trying to distinguish between *goodness* and *success* within the framework of Greek thought. Aristotle wrestled with the idea of *justice* but did not really emerge with a satisfactory notion of *law*. But both had envisaged a general human nature, a universal *reason*, and an ideal of *government* which, in the end, was not merely Greek. The Romans were building an empire within which diverse peoples had somehow to be accommodated. The notion of a *citizenship* which would hold within the empire but which could be obtained according to rules rather than according to birth was essential to them.

Such a system can provide an organization capable of uniting large bodies of men of different persuasions and cultures, particularly when there is some crisis to be faced. The Roman Empire provided, above all, *order* in a disorderly and uncertain world. But for what did men want order?

The older system embodied in primitive Greek democracy had

an obvious and concrete goal — however shallow and silly it might seem when satirized by Plato or analyzed by Aristotle: it aimed at enabling the individual (if that individual was a Greek *and* a citizen!) to do what he pleased. That self-destructive aim was held in check only by local loyalties, ties of family and an inherited sense of community. The Roman world by contrast provided a formal structure which required some self-sacrifice — an agreement not to do those things which impinged on the rights of other Roman citizens as well as a willingness to pay a tax which tended to rise. It created a privileged class of full citizens who could profit from such a system, and a variety of only slightly less privileged classes. But in the name of what, was the self-sacrifice to be made?

In trying to be universal, the empire necessarily lost its close associations with the ideals of its original culture and ultimately provided no content, no concrete goals, no common ends. Epicurus had noted that, failing anything else, men will seek pleasure and avoid pain. It seemed to him that this was the most basic feature of the human situation; but he understood very well that the task of maximizing pleasure and minimizing pain is odd: the best way to maximize your pleasures and minimize your pains is to minimize your desires. For pain consists in some sense of unfulfilled desires and is added to by assorted bodily accidents which become more numerous as one seeks the fancier pleasures. He advocated that one should live on thin gruel and a little goat's cheese.

People do seek pleasure, but have rarely been able to take the advice of Epicurus. The richer Romans eventually did behave like the characters who portray them in Hollywood movies. They indulged their bodily pleasures in ways which still fill the movie houses. But such behaviour hardly invites loyalty, and — what is much more important — the pursuit of pleasure is an endless and unsatisfying task. Jeremy Bentham and John Stuart Mill in the last century advocated a policy of maximizing pleasure and have been widely followed. But you cannot maximize pleasure. The problem is both logical and practical: however much pleasure you have, you can always add some more to it. The quest is endless. Furthermore, adding pleasure gets harder as time goes on. The body tires. Old pleasures may dissipate faster than new ones are added.

But the essence of the matter in Hegel's view is that the Roman empire gave way to the Christian world of the Middle Ages because Christianity provided content to what had been a rather empty and abstract system. Hegel speaks of the "sterile spirit" of Rome. In a way the Roman system defeated itself. As order became better and better established and the legal system grew, the power to keep order became less mysterious and was clearly less valued. Far from a crisis, the abstact system could no longer attract the loyalty of enough people enough of the time. Christianity took over the Empire, most of its titles, much of its organization and, after a while, even its intellectual institutions.

The Church took the Roman idea of law and established its canon law — a law which embodied a concrete and unified set of goals. As the law became concrete, however, it had to take account of specific aims and aversions. It was enriched through the realities of culture and responded to the peculiarities of space and time. Even so, it remained somewhat abstract. It is a long way from primitive Christianity to the Christianity of the High Middle Ages. Romanized, legalized Christianity enshrouded the primitive Christian experience, while the Christian experience gave shape, meaning and content to the abstract law. Hegel speaks of this process as the externalizing of the Christian ideal, and ascribes to it the corruption of the Church before the Reformation. For, once the system is formalized, one is bound by rules, not conscience. If one can foster one's self-advantage within the rules, one may feel no compunction against doing so — as much within the Church as between the Church and its rivals. The unity of Christendom finally broke down. Politically and religiously fragmented, Europe emerged as the modern states we still have with us.

We can explain it this way: the law abstractly is universal. Without concrete aims, it is empty. Yet concrete aims emerge from experiences which are particular, and not as yet perfectly subjected to reason. Furthermore, as with Christianity, the various attempts to impose reason on the structure may be inadequate to the experiences. Thus the ideal law of reason which binds all men may not be forthcoming. Politically, such concrete structures of thought created divisions just because they were particular, tied to the daily experiences of men in one region rather than another. Divisions demand boundaries and boundaries make for disputes.

Hegel could finally see no principle which would clearly transcend the differences inherent in modern states. Hence the possibility of war, irrationality, unresolved conflict. At most, he thought the spirit of the times, whatever it was, would win through. A hundred years later, in Flanders' fields, rather too many of his hinted predictions came true.

Indeed, one can now see what the problem was at the time of the French Revolution: forms of freedom evolve through forms of order. These forms of order are transmitted through institutions. If one sweeps away the institutions, one tends to go back almost to the beginning. One does not go back to what may have been the idyllic tribal state, for that requires a kind of organization which is no longer available. Societies tend, rather, to regress to a kind of primitive competition of the sort which follows the breakdown of tribalism. Since that usually proves intolerable, desperation sets in and one adopts whatever model is most intelligible: the even more despotic pseudo-monarchy of Napoleon.

We can also see, on Hegel's analysis, why events like the First World War might become paralyzing. The structure of the system remains invisible, the institutions do not exist to permit an expression of the responses of the participants. No lines of communication connect a German soldier to a French one.

Thus Hegel's explanation has power, but it is interesting for us to notice that some of his analysis is invalidated by our own experience in Canada. He may have correctly noticed important stages in the historical process; but it is also true that the various phases do not simply disappear. In Canada there are still societies which seek to guard their tribal unity, and there are societies which represent different phases of European history that are not very clearly marked out by Hegel. The differences between the communitarian societies which came with immigrants from Eastern Europe and the industrialized individualism of many American immigrants to Alberta in the late nineteenth and early twentieth century are important, but their nature is not readily explicable by Hegel's analysis. Some of the immigrant groups from eastern Europe — the Doukhobors or the Mennonites, for instance — stem from the left wing of the Reformation, a tendency which sought a deeper notion of community and resisted the individualism which generally went with the breakdown of the Middle Ages. Others came from areas in which feudalism had not really disappeared. Our position is special just because, in addition to the indigenous peoples, we began with groups which to some degree evaded the transformations of mind that had paved the way in seventeenth and eighteenth-century Europe for the final triumph of capitalism in the nineteenth century.

But Hegel does provide the key to a number of our important problems. He calls attention to the problems of complex pluralistic societies which seek their solutions in abstract legal and political systems. It is difficult to be loyal to an abstraction. A modern federal system is exposed to many of the perils of the Roman empire.

If, as is surely the case in Quebec, the specific elements of the culture which generate loyalty are perceived as being regional, there

Public Archives (C87500)   Fainmel, National Film Board, World War II

Marx grasped that, as this artist tries to convince us, management and labour must somehow work together to keep the capitalist system in some kind of equilibrium. But he also realized that capitalist industry is a hot smoking thing which does not rest easily on two hands so obviously from different bodies.

will be a strong tendency toward regional autonomy. Loyalties are generated by shared experiences — the language one speaks, the church one attends (or thinks of oneself as staying away from), the books one reads, the jokes one has heard before. Ultimately, one needs a collective vision and some agreement about how it might eventually be made real. As for federal elections, it may be from the Roman idea of universality that we derive the abstract notion that a vote is a vote, and that any vote can be exchanged for any other. But in a constituency 80% English-speaking and 20% French-speaking, particular votes are not so easily interchangeable.

Marx once claimed to have "stood Hegel on his head." Though he continued to think that human freedom was the central political issue and that it could be provided, as Hegel had thought, only in a community in which there was a genuine sharing of experience and a sense of mutual responsibility, he doubted that one could explain history by reference to the inevitable working out of the idea of freedom. He thought, instead, that social organization depends upon the organization of the means of production. The arrangements for production divide the participants into classes. The capitalist system, for instance, produces wealth from manufacture and trade. Those who own or control the means of production, capitalists, control the society. The producers of this wealth make up the other basic class, the proletariat. Ultimately, according to Marx, the driving force of the system is "surplus value." The real value in the system is what the worker puts into it in the sense that wealth is generated through the transformation of nature by human activity. But the capitalist system complicates that process. Marx describes, in a famous passage in *Capital*, the mysterious process by which the capitalist gets something out of the system which he didn't put in. The worker works all day but gets back only part of what he puts in. The rest goes to the capitalist. All 'real' value comes from the transformation of nature by human effort, yet somehow there is something over for the capitalist investor. Thus the capitalist whose factory makes $100,000 worth of boots and who pays out $90,000 in wages and expenses has made himself $10,000. But he has not, in one sense, added anything to the economy. We can see that sense if we think of it this way: he put $100,000 worth of boots on the market but he has distributed only $90,000 in purchasing power.

If that were the whole of the story, goods would pile up everywhere. Of course, it is not. The $10,000 is usually invested and thus goes back into the economy. But it does represent an empty space in the system. The system must expand to fill it. The invested

$10,000 has to go somewhere. If everyone at home has boots, one must find some bootless people elsewhere and make them wear boots, or one must create new demands, new needs.

Whether the workers or the capitalists profit from all this expansion is less important than the fact that there is no equilibrium in the system. Marx knew, of course, that the pressure to expand is eased by wars which produce and destroy large amounts of non-consumable goods and so act as a substitute for expansion. The pressure can also be eased by public works projects. In our time welfare systems turn citizens into simple consumers who use up a little of the existing surplus without creating a new one.

Since Marx's day, too, there have been important technical changes in the system, especially in the fields of money and banking. These open up new possibilities for controlling the economy. Yet the system never does seem to reach equilibrium and the consequences of even a brief surcease in its expansion are well known to everyone.

The tensions within the system are, obviously, great. But Marx in his earlier writings especially was even more concerned with the way in which such a system impinges on the quality of human life. His critique of Hegel stems not so much from the different analyses they might have given of historical transformations, as from Marx's perception of the way in which changing economic systems twist all the facets of human life.

The "class war" was not just the outcome of the problem of surplus value but of a system which separates the worker from his product, ultimately from his own identity. Hegel had argued that personal identity does not derive from some mysterious inner awareness of ourselves but from reflecting on what we do in the world. To know who you are, you must act and then be able to find yourself in your actions. Marx accepted this proposition, but focussed it specifically in productive labour.

A novelist knows he is a novelist because he, like everyone else, can see what he has produced and, reflecting on it, can ask himself how well it expresses his intent. An artisan similarly can find himself in the piece of furniture he produces, or the stone carving on the cathedral front. The farmer finds traces of himself and of the past generations in the shape of his fields, the stone-work in his barn, the paths he has made and followed all his life. They are his and he can feel at home there. Traditionally, in every occupation, there is some way of 'feeling at home.' Mothers respond to the recognition of their children, or the gradual transformation of their houses into some recognizable pattern. Teachers follow the lives of their students, and so on.

The capitalist system makes labour itself a commodity, and organizes work so that it is frequently very difficult to find the result of one's labour, and so that individuals become units to be trained in a way which permits, over whole industries, anyone to be substituted for anyone else. This creates alienation. Marx followed Hegel in distinguishing two sorts of "alienation," one natural and one not at all natural. The first results from the fact that one must act in order to find oneself in the world. In acting one creates something new — a departure from oneself. On reflection, however, one can fit the new to the old and retain one's view of oneself as a coherent, ongoing person. The second type of alienation occurs when one cannot make the connection, when what one does seems to have no connection with oneself. If most of one's working life is spent producing articles with which one cannot identify oneself and if much of the rest of one's life is passive, one may become an empty cipher. There really is a large population which goes home at night and fills its emptiness with American television and Canadian beer.

Marx as a materialist attacked Hegel as an idealist. What he was concerned about was not just metaphysical materialism — the doctrine that the world is composed of material objects and that men are identical with their own bodies. Engels was a metaphysical materialist in this sense, but what Marx insisted on was more specific — that it is the material conditions of life which control the political and social circumstances.

Thus the possibility of effective cooperative action is frustrated by the fact that capitalism tends to deprive people of effective identities and the simple will power to undertake action. Emptied and tired (and perhaps deafened) the worker *needs* a beer when he gets home, and the prospect of a meeting at the local co-op is about as enticing as the prospect of a meeting of the C.G.I.T or the Orange Lodge. The political system, left to itself, is not so much controlled by capitalists as it is by the problems of the capitalist system. Politicians are constantly taken up with the dizzying swings of an economic system for which there is no equilibrium, and with the instabilities of a world in which there is no prospect of anything but conflict.

This brings us to the crucial question of ideology — Marx's account of the animating ideas of our social and political life. Though, on his view, our political life is, in fact, controlled by its economic substructure, we nonetheless dispute over rival theories which claim to be able to solve problems that are in fact insoluble within the system. We remain unconscious of the real forces at work in our lives. Why?

Marx's thesis was that we are victims of what he called "ideologies". They result from our materially-conditioned perceptions of the social situation, and from our need to idealize these perceptions. A Francophone worker in Quebec may correctly perceive his social situation as one in which he is dominated by bosses who speak English, one in which he must constantly try to be acceptable to another culture. An ideal social situation would be one without *les Anglais*. He becomes a Separatist, developing an ideology that responds to his social situation but which, in itself, is not aimed at changing the economic system underlying his social conditions.

But finally, one must change the economic system. Marx was not very clear (as his critics keep telling us) about just what the new economic system was to be. The reason for this is that his theory is really a theory of history: it seeks to explain, to make us aware of the principles of change, so that we ourselves may then make changes. He did hope, much more strongly than Hegel, that he could foresee the future. What he foresaw was the collapse of the capitalist system in a way which would leave the proletariat in charge. Without an opposing class, the proletariat would become conscious of its natural unity and forge a new economy in which, eventually, the state and even the law would wither away.

The oddity is that this, in its turn, seems a good example of an "ideology". Marx supposes that, beneath the Archie Bunkerish surface of the tired and liverish worker, there lurks the real man; who, without the pressures of the system, would turn out to be honest, friendly, hard-working, and capable of the vast manifold of human capacities. But this does seem to be an idealization. Where the system has been replaced, Hegel has generally proved to be right: In the absence of a firm social structure, one regresses. In the Soviet Union, the collapse of the system led to an inevitable search for a model of public order. The one that was adopted seems to have been the one that people understood — the Czarist bureaucracy. Even private schools developed in Czarist times for the children of the aristocracy were maintained for children of those who had served the party or the state well. Marx's vision of the future has yet to emerge in reality, but it is not merely that vision which raises doubts about the universal applicability of the theory.

Like Hegel, Marx envisaged history as a series of stages each of which replaces the earlier ones. He helps us explain the cultural complexities which we find in Canada by making us notice that the populations effectively transformed by the industrial revolution are different in many ways from those which were not so deeply touched — immigrants from industrialized western Europe are not just like those from the more agricultural eastern Europe. But he did not envisage these populations side by side and his implied solution to the conflict of such peoples with substantial indigenous groups seems to be their assimilation to the pattern of European history. Our nationalist in Quebec is not just in the position which Marx might envisage for him. Never having been effectively transformed by the industrial revolution, he may nourish older and more profound notions of community. He may be able to generate new kinds of order. And, indeed, though it may be a government of tinkerers with the system, many people would agree that the Parti Québécois has provided more humane and effective government than has been seen in Canada for some time.

The conflicts in Canada are not *just* those of the class war. Thus a worker for a locally owned corporation in Quebec may genuinely be torn between his response to the capitalist-labour confrontation and his sense that the employer provides an economic base for the culture and community in which he has his roots. Such complexities have played a large part in the history of Catholic and independent trade unions in Quebec, and the conflict between these unions and the American-dominated "international" unions may be more significant in the long run than the class war itself.

Again, the capitalist system, though it has ravaged the agrarian economies of the prairie provinces on more than one occasion, never quite dominated it. The strength of the co-operative movement is at least a faint echo of an older idea of community. People have not divided easily along class lines. Saskatchewan gave political life to John Diefenbaker. But it also gave political force and life to the C.C.F. and has even given wavering support to the uncertain N.D.P. The same people often seem to have supported both — essentially, because the older communitarianism of Diefenbaker strikes an even deeper chord than the economic analyses of the moderate socialists. More of the structure of this and related problems will emerge as we go along: here the point is simply that the Marxist analysis, intended for the linearly directed societies of western Europe is apt to produce bafflement when applied to Canada.

One should also bear in mind that it is not obvious that what Marx is saying really goes to the root of the matter. Pierre Clastres has argued, for instance, that the breakdown of tribalism cannot really have come about through simple economic causes. The possibility of an economic surplus is not built into tribal societies and without such a surplus the trade and commerce and the social division built on differing ownership of means of production could not come about. But why should one produce a surplus? Why should one be interested in trade? Clastres suggests that demographic features (population pressure for instance) may bring about these changes. But the basic change of outlook involved in the idea that one should produce more than one needs seems hardly possible unless there is some force capable of bringing it about. I have suggested, as I think Hegel would, that tribal societies contain within them a tension created by the fact that individuals exist but are subordinated to a common understanding. Given such a tension, small events may have large consequences. But it is the underlying tension for which we must search. It is not enough just to say that it exists.

Hegel and Marx cast light on our affairs but they, too, turn out to have perspectives which are puzzling and may need explaining by reference to some more fundamental notion. Hegel and Marx both suggested that many of our thoughts do not have the significance they seem to have. The Hegelian thesis that history is often the result of structures hidden from consciousness was taken over by Marx who also added the thesis that we ascribe events to causes dictated by our ideologies. The extreme case of 'idealization' he supposed to be found in religion, in which we project the social structure onto a celestial framework and ascribe to God the feudal system — or the political order in Quebec. Religion was supposed to be the "opiate of the people" not because people were doped by priests but because people use religion as a psychological substitute for reality, or confuse idealized perceptions with real ones.

Hegel and Marx thus struck deeply at the enlightenment notion that we can reform the world by reason alone, and opened up the idea of the unconscious — a notion which derives largely from the German philosopher Leibniz in the seventeenth century, and from Immanuel Kant's successor Johann Friedrich Herbart, who was born at the end of the eighteenth century. Sigmund Freud, however, gave the unconscious even harder work to do.

Freud began by suggesting what everyone would acknowledge: civilization itself requires a re-organization of basic human drives. We must suppress much of our natural inclination in order to have a civilization at all. The very notion of an order supposes a limitation on some activities in order to stimulate others, though such an arrangement might be wholly voluntary. The question which he posed, however, was: what happens then?

The answer in his view is that these surface changes do not bring about a real change in underlying human nature. What civilization makes us reject by way of conscious thought is merely buried in the subconscious. A great part of what is suppressed is sexual. Another part of what is suppressed, Freud thought, as he grew older, is the death wish. There is in us a natural tension of forces, a competition of life and death. Civilization orders our sexual lives and suppresses our thoughts of death — for, though people come and go, societies continue indefinitely. Death is a disruptive, a social phenomenon to be thrust out of sight.

But, though death and sex are subjected to social controls and rituals, they colour everything in sight. They may result in any amount of confused squabbling and scrambling of our surface life. The real direction persists in the unconscious. Freud peopled the unconscious with a variety of characters — personified principles if you like — which rejoiced in such names as Id, Ego and Superego. These characters fed on the materials received from the conscious life and nourished rich affairs of their own, usually safely out of sight. Indeed, the conscious life is a kind of screen on which is flashed messages which represent the manoeuverings amongst and between them. Even the Ego, which represents conscious self-awareness, really feeds, Freud said, on the materials of the unconscious.

Freud, like Spinoza, thought that one had more or less to come to terms with one's inner life and that the turmoil of the world could not really be brought to an end except, perhaps, in so far as individuals could be helped to understand their own unconscious minds. The only way to accomplish this is to undergo the process of psychoanalysis, and that can be done only by an analyst and a patient working as a pair over a very long period. The social cost of psychoanalyzing the whole populace would be astronomical.

Freud thought that the passage from tribalism to individuality was a violent one, probably a good deal more dramatic than anything Hegel or Marx thought of. The emergence of the individual and the breakdown of the paternal authority is a kind of murder, symbolic or real. The demand to be free in that sense is a demand to dominate.

Symbolically, this expresses a tension which is in all of us. If it cannot be resolved — and human nature in Freud's view remains fixed and basic desires can only be suppressed — must it not ultimately erupt in violence? The violence might be that of crime, of a wave of meaningless anarchist acts, or of large scale wars. Our violent sports recall our inner tensions, while our religions celebrate deicide and the guilty hope of resurrection.

Violence on such a view would not be finally eradicable, and we may suppose that, as society becomes more and more sophisticated, more and more of our natural drives will have to be suppressed. According to Freud they can be sublimated — their energy released for other purposes — yet even that transformation always creates a tension.

If Freud is right, we must expect that a technological society like ours with the power to destroy everyone will, in due course, succeed in doing so. For there is little chance that the underlying tensions can be resolved by psychoanalysis. We only keep the insane asylums from filling up by blasting minds with electricity or doping them. But we cannot lock up, drug and electrify enough people to do much about the larger tensions.

On this view, of course, Hegel and Marx are rationalizing, just as the practitioners of religion rationalize. Hegel explains the tension and the violence as the working out of an idea. Marx explains it as a conflict in the economic order. But, to a Freudian, it is really more immutable than that.

The progression from Hegel to Marx to Freud and beyond parallels the growing stresses and strains of the industrial revolution and its aftermath. As the pressures grew, as more and more seemingly irrational acts occurred — wars, revolutions, waves of crime, anarchist bombings, the stockpiling of weapons capable of destroying us — more and more drastic theories have been advanced.

It is intriguing to apply Marx's theory of ideology to Freud. Freud treated mainly middle-class patients in turn-of-the-century Vienna. His clients were people with relative freedom and often with significant power of their own. They were 'free' in the terms which they generally understood. Though their lives were in fact confined to a kind of elaborate ritual dance, they seemed to themselves to have chosen to do most of the things they did. They appeared in some sense to be able to do almost anything they wanted. But the conditions of their social position inhibited them. Even more than the working class they were expected to confine their sex lives to the accepted channels. What they were unconscious of was the source of their desire to conform to the social order. One wonders whether, if Freud had practiced in rural Manitoba, he would have attached the same weight to sexual instinct. Perhaps people embroiled in more pressing worries have less to bury.

It could be argued that Freud perceived a social situation,

imagined what it would be like to have its pressures removed, grasped that such removal would disable that society, and created a picture of what it would take to have adequate self-understanding and *acceptance* of the social order. He was surely right in the sense that people can easily be motivated by appeal to their sexual instinct, as almost any advertisement proves; but that, too, supposes the kind of society in which people are free enough from other pressures (*and* empty enough of other ideas) to be motivated in that way.

But the notion that under our surface consciousness the *real* cast of characters — Id, Ego, and Superego — play out an endless drama in which our consciousness is mainly a kind of stage lighting is, in the end, bizarre. Though "consciousness is attached to the Ego" in "its relation to the Id it is like a man on horseback." "The Ego uses borrowed forces;" it has none of its own. But the Ego must not only ride the Id, the subconscious forces of natural desire; it must also contend with the Superego, the "Ego ideal."

Freud's Id, Ego, and Superego are personified principles as were Aquinas's angels, and in some sense such principles *are* undoubtedly at work in us. Everyone has had experience of being torn by rival principles or of feeling that an argument is going on inside, and every sensible person acts, much of the time, from principle. Freud is alleging of course that the principles which we use consciously are not our 'real' principles. Rather, the Id, the Ego and the Superego are like actors who can assume many parts, and we are often deceived. Beneath the surface play, in fact, is another one. The drama in the unreachable depths of the unconscious is very limited and represents perhaps the dreariest stage play since the Middle Ages. If their parts were acted out on stage one would have, indeed, a mediaeval morality play — desire pitted against ambition, and ambition against moral principle.

Freud is confronting man after the industrial revolution. Western man has been depersonalized, substantially emptied out, trapped in conflicts and rituals which no longer have much meaning for him. It is this loss of meaning in life which both Hegel and Marx were also trying to understand. Freud, too, is part of what needs to be explained. Again, applied to our own affairs, we can see something of his relevance.

But we cannot just pick and choose between Freud, Hegel, and Marx. Each illumines some features of our lives. If we look nearer to home in our search for a theory we may find more focussed light. The Canadian theorist Harold Innis came, near the end of a short but hectic career in public and academic life in Toronto and Ottawa, to question the fundamental claims to knowledge which underlie the modern social sciences. He had been trained in philosophy, abandoned it as "dead and stuffed" (especially at the University of Toronto), studied economics, and gradually became a social historian. He did not skip lightly across the academic lines (and sometimes took refuge in his status as an economist) but, as he moved, it became clear to him that each discipline tended to represent not just rival ways of thinking about things which might have their source in the jostlings of the academy, but rival interests. I can put it no better than Robin Neill does in *A New Theory of Value, The Canadian Economics of Harold Innis*: "As Innis understood it, each branch of social science developed under the protection of some institution whose existence it rationalized." The theory was only sketched. Innis never arrived at a final form of it.

Hegel, Marx and Freud set out to criticize the basic structure of interests which underlies each of their various disciplines — history, economics, and psychology. All three have been received by the official academy with a certain suspicion. Yet each remained tied to the point of view which enveloped the disciplines. Each tried to find a new way of putting that point of view, but none of them escaped entirely from its limitations. Each sought to explain the human condition and therefore history. Hegel uses the original discipline, the history of ideas and its attendant metaphysics as an entry into political theory. Marx tries to undercut political theory by showing that its base is in economics. Freud tries to undercut both political theory and economics by showing that their base lies in psychology.

If we were to look, in Innis's way, for the institutions which the discipline of history originally served, we would find surely that history served both Church and State as a source of legitimacy. History became important as a discipline at the time of the Reformation when the Church needed to rebut claims about its legitimacy, to sustain the belief that it continued to carry the original Christian doctrine, that its officers got their authority at the end of an unbroken chain which stretched back to Christ. But a weapon used for defence can also be used for attack.

In the battle of historians Hegel appears as the successor to Vico and Kant in a progression of sophisticated attempts to produce a theory that might arbitrate the dispute. History served the State in the same way — as part of the search for legitimacy in power. Again, Hegel appears as a mediating force in the battle, trying to tie history to a principle — the development of freedom — and providing a base for the arguments about what legitimacy might consist of.

But history is more than this. It also studies human actions, considered as actions of individuals, not as economic forces, psychological drives or whatever. It is in a certain sense the most traditional of the social sciences. Indeed, it has been the definer of tradition. History continues also to be involved in story-telling and, in telling good stories, conveys the belief that what individuals do matters. Indeed, a good story needs a hero or a villain — a king, a general, a con-man, a scheming politician, even an enigmatic Mackenzie King.

Looked at from this background we can see the ambiguity of Hegel's programme: he sought to defend history as a discipline by giving it a theory, but he also transformed it into the study of impersonal forces. He argued that the idea of freedom forms human life and dominates history. He thus opened the door to a kind of impersonal explanation of human behaviour, to the transformation of the study of man from the personal to the impersonal. Yet he wants to appear as the defender of freedom, a freedom which cannot really exist if we are the victims of impersonal forces. Clearly, this ambiguity itself stems from the conditions of the time, from the new science and the technology which made possible the industrial revolution and which demanded impersonal explanations on the one hand and, on the other, from social conditions which made it possible, more than ever, to envisage a whole free man with enough power to instantiate, finally, the possibilities of the human animal.

Hegel is standing between these forces. But his work manifests something else as well. It suggests, though he shies away from saying it, that history is a continuous progress into the future. If so, heaven is in the future on earth and not in another realm. The pressure of science and technology as demystifying agents tended, then as now, to undercut the transcendent notion of another world, and the easiest substitute is to hold that the ideal world is immanent in this one. Hegel would finally, I think, have battled against this replacement; but it is interesting that it is latent in his philosophy.

Marx turns away from Hegel by substituting economics for intellectual history. In so doing, he sides with those who are challenging the old power: Church and State drew their notions of legitimacy from historical continuity. The challengers wanted to show that legitimacy depended upon correctness of economic theory, not just history. If we look at economics in this way — suggested by Innis — Marx is in fact engaged in the same enterprise as Adam Smith. Of course Marx would insist that he is defending a class interest, the interest of the proletariat. Adam Smith used economics directly to undercut political theory in a way which exactly served the interest of the new controllers of economic power who wanted to master the political situation, Marx saw through the guise.

But the new system did more than dethrone the old aristocracy. Even Adam Smith argued that the system would have to be controlled. Without regulation of the banking system, he argued, the capitalist system would certainly collapse. And he realized that commerce requires a whole range of public services. The time was one of the rapid growth of bureaucracy, and the interaction of that growing bureaucracy and the merchant class is, in itself, a fascinating story. They go together. The new wealth supports a larger apparatus of State and creates conflicts. The system fed empires and created armies on a scale hitherto unknown. One who attacks the old system in the name of economics, therefore, must, if he questions the legitimacy of the merchant and the manufacturer, improve the prospects of the bureaucrat.

If Smith is the friend (though a carefully cautious one) of the merchant princes, Marx is the prophet (though a still more cautious one) of the bureaucrat. True, he thinks the state will finally wither away — *if* the system is allowed to work its own way to the end. But before that happens there will be much work for bureaucrats. There is the transition phase which Marx called "the dictatorship of the proletariat." This is a period in which the class-conscious and enlightened part of the working class must take over and plan for the coming communist state. Who are these 'class-conscious' far-seeing men and women?

Marx, after all, exhibits the same ambiguity as Hegel: he seems to be talking about individual freedom, but in fact, he talks of impersonal forces and how they are to be organized. Marx too is trying to assimilate the transcendent to the immanent. Heaven is in the workers' paradise, never well specified but lying, somehow, on the other side of the bureaucratic purgatory.

If Marxist economics and Smith's economics represent two sides of an interest conflict, it remains true that they do not represent *all* the interests in hand. Economics concerns the public side of the life of the classes which were triumphant in the industrial revolution. But there is, as with Hegel's concept of the Idea, a private side as well. One might argue that psychology in the nineteenth century developed as a response to problems which were worsening as that inner side decayed. Marxist materialism in denying the primacy of that inner side is, of course, also proclaiming the importance of economics over psychology.

If, as Hegel and Marx had argued, however, the industrial revolution had cut men loose from themselves, had created an endless series of identity crises, it might be expected that problems would result in the inner lives of men and women. The poor could soak themselves in gin and the rich often blew their minds with opium, but something more dignified was needed. It was called psychology.

Such an enterprise is suspect. For what it does is to find therapies that cover up the disasters of the system. Instead of taking away the pressures which drive men out of their minds, we seek to change their minds. But Freud, one must remember, was still battling against the notion that problems of the mind are something unnatural. As a first step toward a humane outlook he hoped to integrate mental disturbance into the natural order and, indeed, he began with the notion that one might integrate psychology and physiology. In this he evidently succeeded.

But his theory, from the perspective of one looking at the social system as a whole, remains suspect. For the purpose of his therapy is to become reconciled. It is argued that civilization necessarily creates discontents, but that the solution is internal to consciousness. It is an alternative to changing the system. In practice, psychoanalysis is mostly available to the rich, making it more than ever the servant of the institutions which spawned it. More orthodox psychology escaped somewhat from this charge by following Freud's earlier bent, aligning itself with physiology and so with the natural sciences, and by seeking to provide universal truths and conditioning techniques available to be used on the masses. In so doing it became open to abuse in quite other ways.

Like Marx and Hegel, Freud is also involved in the central ambiguity. For personal action and responsibility by whole individuals, we substitute the mythical Id, Ego, and Superego. In the name of personal integrity, we replace the person by impersonal forces. Only the privileged few, who encounter a good analyst and have the time and the money, may recover even some of what they have lost. And, like Hegel and Marx, Freud is involved in the shift from the transcendent to the immanent. The angels and devils of Thomas Aquinas are now within us, infinitely duller, and locked in endless wrangle. It is unimaginable, in Freud's view of the world, that they might break free again.

Two issues remain dominant: the more crucial is about how we can manage to understand our condition without shifting the burden of responsibility onto impersonal forces which, even when they are recognized, cannot ultimately be controlled. Logically, appeal to such forces is suspect: if they really control us, how is it that we can trust our beliefs about them or about anything else? For, then, our beliefs will be the result of these forces; our mental deliberations will be a trial before a bought jury. The second issue is the problem of reconciling our view of the world with the idea of the transcendent. The transcendent, we are learning, will not go away. It comes back harmlessly as Mackenzie King's spooks, or not so harmlessly as the fundamentalism of Ayatollah Khomeini, Jimmy Carter and Menachem Begin. If reason cannot encompass the experiences which sustain it, the transcendent may be more dangerous than the atomic bomb.

We must be able to bring history back to consciousness in a way which does not destroy our integrity and shift the burden for ever onto forces that no one can control. And we must also try to construct a whole human life, at least as rich as the one before the industrial revolution, hopefully far better.

Chapter 5

Shared Identities

C anada is a curious kind of time machine: we can travel across our own country and find societies belonging to various phases of western civilization together with indigenous societies which belong to wholly different time frames. Our kind of pluralism represents a temporal order in which one phase is not necessarily simply replaced by another but rather encapsulated. We have in Canada preserved certain features of human history which were largely obliterated in Europe. If history is carried around in the structures of our experience, we may have more of it than our European ancestors. They have the buildings and the monuments. But we have some of the communities more or less intact. C.S. Lewis liked to say that he was one of the last living specimens of Old Western man. I dare say we have quite a few of them left in Canada. And there are still those amongst us who carry with them first hand experience of the tribal life of which even Plato could only dream.

In an individualistic age, this commitment to an organic society has been enough to make a difference which can be noticed. Yet our variety of diversities has been sufficient to convince us, beyond much doubt, that a specifically Canadian cultural pluralism exists. This pluralism has led to weak and divided commitments to our institutions. Often indeed to commitments divided between our own institutions and those of the surrounding or earlier societies to which they have had close ties. But it has also led to a demand for institutions which can recognize and cope with plurality itself. It is because of this that we must now look deeper into the question of how communities are formed — to ask, finally, of what they consist and how it can be that they can become involved in plurality in the way in which we find them.

If one asks "what are societies composed of ?" the obvious answer is "people." The answer is obvious, but not necessarily informative. It is like saying "people are composed of cells and cells are composed of chemicals, therefore people are composed of chemicals." That too is true, again not very informative. One may suspect that the laws of psychology are not, after all, those of chemistry. Even between chemistry and physics there is a difference, and between chemistry and biology, for all the advances of bio-chemistry, there is again a difference. There are developmental laws in biology which do not seem to have counterparts in inorganic chemistry. So far as inorganic chemistry is concerned, elements can be compounded, dispersed and compounded again. The rules work both ways. But when we get to a living thing like a moth, the developmental laws are influenced by the direction of time, you cannot turn the moth back into the caterpillar again. It seems even more true that any account of child development involves developmental laws that are not readily reversible.

A human person is a different *kind* of thing than a collection of atoms and molecules, if only because personality is itself a relational notion. I know who I am because there are other people with whom I can contrast myself and in relation to whom I establish my identity.

Hegel had noticed that if you try to think about yourself you eventually come up with a blank. Thinking about oneself seems easy. But try to think about the self which is thinking about yourself. When you think about 'yourself,' you are really reflecting on what you have done in the world — on the events of your life, the people you have known, the things you have seen. The self which does all this only exists as a term in this relation. It is a kind of empty shell, the universal 'form' which experience can take, something Immanuel Kant had called the "transcendental ego." As such, your "pure ego" is just the same as everyone else's. What distinguishes you from me is very largely our social relationship.

Indeed, I suppose that, if I were the only person in the world, I would have great difficulty even distinguishing myself *from* the world. Should I say that the whole world is my own experience? If I were alone in the world it would seem to be so. How would I know where I began and the world outside ended? I might distinguish myself by saying "well, if I stick a pin in it and it hurts, then it's me and if it doesn't, then it's the outside world." But even that doesn't work very well. It doesn't hurt if you stick pins in your toenails or cut your hair.

As a matter of fact, it's not a very good idea to try to identify yourself by reference to your body at all. Bits of it can now be replaced. Someday, perhaps, all of it can be replaced. (What if we are able to reproduce the electro-chemical patterns and the structure of your brain on a newly manufactured one? You'll still *think* it's you.) Even now, if a person changes enough we may be prepared to say that he's someone else. (Can one really be "born again"?) In law, identity is a matter for the jury to decide — not a matter of principle. And we may be prepared to admit that there are cases of multiple personality.

These possibilities may seem bizarre: but they underline the fact that everyone has come to realize in our time: personal identity *is* problematic.

John Watson, a Scotsman who came to Canada five years after confederation and played a central role in Canadian academic affairs almost until his death in 1939, grasped that fact and made it the key problem in his philosophy long before it became fashionable. He insisted that it is nonsense to ask who and what we are unless we remember that we understand ourselves in and through our relations with other people and things. To know who I am, I must be able to express myself in a very complex social structure which serves to differentiate me from everyone else. Indeed, it is only in an historical process in which opportunities exist for marked individual differentiation that our modern notions of personal identity can take root. Individualism is a late-developing political doctrine because it simply would not be intelligible, except in a world in which people felt themselves very distinct and very different from everyone else. This differentiation requires a long history in which what Watson liked to call the "accumulated experience of the (human) race" has been preserved to provide the possibilities for social complexity. This experience can, of course, be used deliberately to create one possibility or another by way of social organization.

Notice the distinction: the accumulated experience of mankind is valuable because men find their individuality in the context of complex cultures. But the transmission of this experience depends upon a variety of institutions. Both Watson and another Scots-born Canadian philosopher, John Clark Murray, insist that though the individual depends both upon history and upon specific social arrangements which can be chosen, and although he ought not to display the arrogance of supposing that he could be himself without the others, the individual nevertheless has, in his community, a measure of freedom to construct or reconstruct his society. Watson in his book *The State in Peace and War* and Murray in his ironically entitled *The Industrial Kingdom of God* (which is only now being published) paint the human condition as one in which something can be done *beyond* the Marxist notion that one should work to speed up the inexorable forces of history, or the Hegelian notion

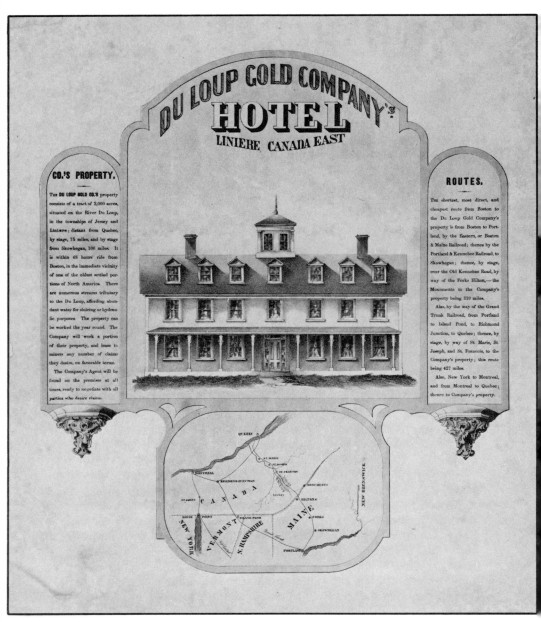

"Societies are not just aggregates of individuals . . ." The Du Loup Gold Company's Hotel promised a man a place in a tidy organization. But the artist grasped that such a social space is apt to end abruptly: The hotel is surrounded by nothing at all.

that one should come to understand how the idea of freedom can work itself out.

From Watson's and Murray's viewpoint, one can see that the capacity to differentiate oneself leaves open a variety of possibilities. The community can express itself through more than one institution even without any change in community structure or technology. But this does not just happen. Buried in ideas like Watson's notion of accumulated human experience is the fundamental concept of culture. For any freedom of action to occur, the culture has to be malleable enough to accommodate a change of ideas, the technology has to be able to make the new ideas feasible, and the community has to be rich enough in its power of making distinctions to be able to provide new ones. At any given moment, many options are closed by history. There is little chance of establishing the practice of head hunting in Ottawa — even in the Tory Party. It collides at too many points with established beliefs and institutions. But other options are open. Despite the enormous pressures of industrial capitalism, it is possible to expand the cooperative movement or to establish a publicly-owned energy industry.

Societies are not just aggregates of individuals. For individuality comes about through social differentiation — the society and its history are primary in the sense of providing the possibility for that differentiation. Yet at the same time societies are not simply inevitable outcomes of a historical process, as Marx sometimes seems to imply, and as Hegel on more than one occasion incautiously claimed. Societies are networks within which individuality can appear. The variables of history and choice have a certain measure of independence.

Murray, who came to Canada in his youth ten years before Watson, was aware that the collective experience which we share with the English, the Scots, the Irish, the French and the Americans is, in addition to being part of the general experience of the human race, so closely intertwined as to form a subset of human experiences which make another kind of unity. He felt at home vacationing in Scotland, lecturing at McGill, or giving a public address at Cooper Union in New York. Yet for him that collective experience was capable of being transformed so as to make a distinctive Canadian society. History is not, after all, linear, and the accumulated experience is only a dead weight if it is unconscious. Murray was as convinced as Marx that the economic substructures of society tend to dominate their political superstructures. Yet he supposed that those, in their turn, were also the products of our beliefs.

Property, for example, is an idea. Murray thought Proudhon had exaggerated when he said that "property is theft." One might argue that first of all the property-owner owes his very individuality to the community in which he finds himself. And then one might argue that property itself is only possible when there are law courts and documents and social arrangements which are generally observed. Thus one who keeps his property to the exclusion of all others does arrogate to himself more than he can possibly be entitled to. Murray would point out, however, that this does not take away all of the property owner's claim. Perhaps, indeed, the property owner did work, and did use the intelligence for which the community had made a place. On this basis Murray proposes a scheme for a cooperative state based on controlled capitalism. Watson advocates a more conservative welfare state. But notice that the argument for either emerges simply by juxtaposing concepts already deeply entrenched in the culture.

Both thinkers recognized that it would take time to bring about such changes. Murray became known as a champion of education for women, while Watson's pupils were a major force in shaping our civil service. Indeed, we have already met many of the demands which Murray and Watson would have made on society, even if we have depersonalized it to a degree which they would have thought intolerable. Our society, evidently, is not frozen.

The problems which constitute our crisis of community stem from the tendency for the culture to fragment and create antagonisms as a response to forces conceived as dominating — and actually made so — by the individualist idea of private property which is built into many of our institutions, together with a failure to grasp the extent to which individual beneficiaries of the system depend for their very identity on the whole community. Some of these problems are, indeed, fairly intractable if viewed in conventional terms: the capitalist system has tended to gather people in very large groups and to leave other parts of the terrain relatively uninhabited. But a country like Canada can offer an intelligible context for human life. For it does provide opportunities which are scaled to the modern conception of human skills and professional diversification. Communities which function must be neither too large not too small. Such opportunities require a culture which surely must be wider than Alberta, or Prince Edward Island, or Ontario.

Yet to differentiate oneself, one needs to know the others

involved in the process. The citizen of southern Ontario who has enriched himself at the expense of the Albertan (or more recently vice-versa) does not in fact grasp that the culture which has made his life intelligible extends far beyond Ontario — or Alberta — and that its failure from poverty in some other region would deprive him equally. He may think that if the Canadian context of social belief fails, he can always find another to take its place, but he reckons without the dimension of scale and the simple fact that he probably does belong to the Canadian culture.

The size and scale of Canadian society is probably within the fairly narrow limits in which such schemes work, although it is frequently negated by considerations which we impose upon it. We imagine ourselves effective parts either of a system too small to do its work or too vast and distant for us to find a place in it. A meeting of Canadians in a professional group or a national trade union is one in which one can expect to play a significant role. A meeting of a comparable group of Manitobans, by contrast, will often contain too few people to provide the necessary range of interests. At the other extreme, it is only rarely, if ever, that a Canadian steel worker can expect to have any influence at all on his union brothers in the United Steel Workers of America. More importantly, if there really is a Canadian context of social belief, the likelihood is that Canadians meeting in such groups will share enough common outlooks to be able to get on with their work.

Evidently, though, we are not strongly enough convinced that we understand this common outlook to know just how to use it to accommodate an intelligible unity in diversity. But we must do so if we are to develop plans for action against our present threatening environment. The theory of mutual identity and dependence must be explicated in a pattern of shared social belief. If one denies that there is a Canadian context of belief and insists that there are really in Canada two (or several) solitudes, then one will tend to think that Quebec or some other region is a unit with the right scale.

But given the Canadian context, a study of the writings of Murray and Watson does suggest a kind of theory about the roots of the relation of individual and community — a theory which, hopefully, is capable of explaining both how our problems come about and how it is that we may have at least some hope of doing something about them. Centrally, it differs from the theories of Marx and Hegel in that it suggests that, as the crucial social concepts come to light and as the reflected identities of others enter into consciousness, a community can free itself, to some extent at least, from its historical determinants. At the same time it differs profoundly from the individualist theories about 'breaking free' in that it is, evidently, the whole community which must break the bonds. It is a community understanding of mutual relations which one must seek, not the private increase in understanding which the Freudian psychoanalysts or the purveyors of enlightenment-style eighteenth-century knowledge imagined.

This at once poses questions about the nature of knowledge itself. This was the problem which so greatly exercised Harold Innis in his last years, and the problem which threatens to checkmate any social theory: for, if knowledge itself is conceived in such a way as to play into the hands of the existing social structure, no increase in knowledge can bring with it the possibility of reform.

On the theory of mutual identity — the kind of theory advanced by thinkers like Watson and Murray — the sort of knowledge which counts in understanding our social situation arises from a conceptual structure that makes possible the analysis. This, itself, comes about from a philosophical reflection on the social situation. This makes philosophy (at least in one of its senses) crucial to any community, and also makes it important that philosophy should actually reflect on the specifics of the culture in which it finds itself. But equally important is the kind of knowledge which comes from awareness of the culture. This is essentially the knowledge of the literary critic, the art historian, and the historian of ideas.

Such claims are difficult to sustain because this type of knowledge does not, by definition, tie in very closely with the power structure of a society. The literary critic, if he does his job honestly is forming a viewpoint which is not one of the viewpoints of the competitors for power — for he is, in Matthew Arnold's sense, whether he likes it or not, putting together the pieces of imaginative understanding. When they are put together they become a shareable whole. The critic can serve the power structure only by dishonesty — only by ignoring some of what is there or by putting it together in a deliberately unintelligible whole. The art historian is in the same position. The historian of ideas knows too much. He can always be an embarrassment to the politician who is embroiled in whatever ideas are sweeping the hustings this week.

Our views of these cultural matters determine what else we think is important. Our outlook on the universe comes from our literature and our philosophy, and it is this outlook which determines whether we casually choose to remanufacture our genes or invest in the latest device for blowing up the world. But of course it is the power structure and the economic organization which is apt to determine whether or not such enquiries are possible.

Chapter 6

Cultures, Communities, and the Basis of Diversity

Is there a passage between the two solitudes?

*I*n an ordinary conversation, the words that we use are all (or nearly all) in the dictionary. These we have in common. When we talk to each other, however, the occasion is unique. It is this conversation, here and now, which counts, and this use of the words has to be distinguished from all the others. The speakers emerge in the conversation out of the particular pattern of words and the direction the conversation takes. Notice how easily you can tell that you are speaking to one of the telephone company's recordings: the recording cannot individuate itself by leading the conversation along a path which marks out *this* occasion from all others.

We are inclined to think of the speakers whose identities are established in conversation as simply existing in a pre-determined way. And they do already exist in some obvious sense. The person you talk to on the telephone was not created by your phone call. But, of course, he is changed a little. And he has grown into what he is through a long slow process characterized by these encounters.

The materials are not all in the language. The culture is vastly more extensive — including gestures, rituals, artifacts, objects of art and the patterns of belief around which experience is normally structured. But it is essentially through objects which are capable of expressing meaning that individuation takes place.

The basic level is therefore a community of meaning. As such, it tends to have two poles. One pole centres on those with whom one is in immediate contact — a family, the neighbours, the experience which is shaped by domestic architecture and the meaningful objects which surround us. In one sense, this is *the* community. For it is here that one meets the situation within which one can express oneself. One may think of this pole as being composed of immediate experiences, each so individual and distinct that it requires an effort to see the pattern of culture within it. But each of the bearers of meaning — words, gestures, tools, the calendar on the wall — leads potentially beyond the immediate. The other pole is given by the limit of the range of these meanings. The word 'ball' may first be taken as a kind of name, the name of the thing with which one plays. But any child can quickly extend it to the next ball. He is quickly equipped with a range of meanings which enable him to walk out of his neighbourhood and to make sense of what he finds downtown. We are constantly engaged in this process of testing and extending the limits of meaning. The child is happy and lucky if he knows that 'jackpine' is a word for a special kind of tree. The poet can invest it with a whole range of further meanings. The tree which the painter puts on canvas has significance beyond the pattern in the paint. The search for the limits towards which that significance can be pushed is amongst the natural preoccupations of the painter.

The search for the limits of this further pole is, after all, what we call curiosity. Whatever curiosity did to the cat, it is inevitable in human beings or in any other creatures who make use of meanings. For meanings carry us beyond their immediate objects.

The limits of all of these meanings, of course, constitute a system in which all the possibilities of human life are instantiated. As meanings are extended they clash, and the clash creates the demand for a systematization which will ultimately reconcile the conflicts. There is thus (as Northrop Frye would have it) a central myth in human life which concerns the great quest and its final attainment in a realm beyond contradiction. The myth is everywhere we look — in religion, art, literature, political utopias and fortune tellers' dreams.

In our more limited reality, however, communities close around temporary limits of meaning. Not all the words and gestures and in-jokes extend beyond the family. The limits of the language itself pose natural limits to the range of the external community. Short of that, political unities with their bureaucratic and legal systems and their much wider codes of customary behaviour set limits to the range within which words and actions have their customary meanings. Some celestial language may unite all men but, if spoken at all, it is spoken only by angels and heard only by natural lyricists like Robert Schumann (whom the music drove mad) or John Keats, for whom truth merged with beauty and beauty with truth.

The range of shared meanings may lead us to legitimize a variety of institutions. In cases like ours, in which large elements in our lives are shared with other cultures, they may allow us to lend our support to a great variety of conflicting institutions.

Meanings spread and genuine individuals are created in this process of inter-change. But the creation of an ideology which has gone with the capitalist economic system, an ideology based on the notion that the public good is best furthered by the independent ownership of the means of production and an economy that maximizes competition, works against the spread of meanings. Individuals isolated from each other and whole classes isolated from other classes are driven to interiorize their meanings and ultimately to communicate much of the time in formal and abstract technical language which is designed, precisely, not to yield to particular occasions. Thus most encounters between human beings in shops, factories, schools, and political meetings consist of the interchange of meaningless formulae — and Matthew Arnold's ideal of a culture that would unite all classes is written off as a madman's dream lest, in effect, it render the system impossible.

In Canada, although the capitalist economic system came to us, the individualist ideology did not — at least not wholly. What we continued to generate, at least in part, was the ideology of the organic society. We did so, of course, in the context of two languages, two sets of institutions, two of almost everything.

At first sight it seems improbable that anything like a common philosophy could underly these two cultures. Indeed, an extreme form of the 'two solitudes' thesis has it that "the most resounding note in our history (is) the juxtaposition of two civilizations, two philosophies, two contradictory views of the nature of man." These words of Professor A.R.M. Lower express a widely held belief, and if they are combined with John Stuart Mill's claim that "among a people without fellow-feeling, especially if they speak different languages, the united public opinion necessary to the working of representative government cannot exist," they seem to bode ill for our future.

If we have two different philosophies, two contradictory views of the nature of man, they ought to show themselves clearly in our social philosophizing. And so they do at a certain level. In the hundred years after 1850 the mainstream of philosophy in English-speaking Canada was more often than not Hegelian, while in French-speaking Canada it was usually Thomist. Mgr Louis-Adolphe Pâquet, the great defender of orthodoxy in Quebec whose influence extended almost up to our times denounced those whom he took to be "Hegelians," including John Watson by name. On the other side, in Toronto, George Brett, an Oxford-educated Englishman who came to us by way of India, was less than enthusiastic about Thomism. But Brett, though no Orangeman, was also no Hegelian. The real Hegelians, especially George Blewett, the most important of the University of Toronto idealists, and Watson himself were not usually hostile to Thomism. Indeed, Mgr Pâquet conceded that Watson took Thomism seriously.

If we look at two of our most serious political philosophers — John Watson and Louis Lachance — we will find Canadian influences at work in the development of the theories to which they were drawn, and also find that these influences worked in the direction of a common understanding. Lachance was much younger than Watson, but the two men wrote major works in social and political philosophy only seventeen years apart, and their lives overlapped by more than forty years. Each, too, had religious affiliations of the sort which are often imagined to be at the roots of the two philosophies. Lachance was a member of the Dominican Order, while Watson was a moving force behind the creation of the United Church of Canada.

Admittedly, each had a more than usually sensitive awareness of the objections which might be made to the tradition to which he belonged and a keen sense of the dangers of over-reaction against the individualism of modern thought. But to say this is just to note that each of them was a discerning observer of the problems of his place and time. And one could compare others on each side — John Clark Murray with Charles de Koninck for instance — with similar results. Watson and Lachance have at least three themes in common: *1.* Each was concerned to bring his tradition to bear on problems about nationalism. *2.* Each objected to a kind of individualism which he thought destructive and each wanted to find a way of combatting it while defending a strong position on human rights. *3.* Each was concerned with the problem of maintaining a society with a strong sense of tradition and continuity without preventing essential social change.

As communities begin to coalesce around common institutions and begin to strike the limits to which they can extend their understandings, fairly large groupings with a solid centre of agreements and a periphery that shades into other cultures is almost inevitable. It is almost inevitable because individuation takes place at close quarters and the pole of the process characterized by powerful feelings and images anchors that individuation to a place and time. Since meanings extend beyond the immediate, neighbouring cultures are always apt to overlap, and zones of uncertainty which can never quite be overcome develop as a result.

In his study of nationalism and religion, Lachance faced a characteristic problem. Religion, the religion to which he devoted his life, claimed universality, and, indeed, characteristically centred on that region of meaning which most obviously does transcend the particular. Yet nationalism was a necessary element in the defence of a humanistic culture which, for him, stood between us and complete defeat by the mechanical monsters of modern capitalism.

In any case, he argued, nationalism performs a basic function: it creates a unity among men and women. It is important because, without it, the social bond in modern times is so weak as to make the search for the common good futile. With it, there is a chance that each of us can transcend his individual pettiness. There is only one human nature, he argued, but there are real national identities which result from parallel developments. The route to the common good is not the same for everyone.

Patriotism is an attachment to a place. A culture is a form of authority, and provides the form of nationalism that is most acceptable. The real unity, however, is not to be ignored. Christianity regards man as one. It is the point of the incarnation to bring us back "into the orbit" of God. This apparent confrontation between universal human nature, the universal religion and the divisions of nationality can, however, be adjudicated if we consider the problem in its historical perspective.

Lachance, as a Christian, sees man in terms of the Fall, as dispersed across the world and at odds with himself. But he says that, from the perspective of Christianity, there is a moment in history when man is pulled toward the centre. But he is pulled back from his own place in an historical context. There may be one goal but many paths. Men are not to be expected to find their way one by one but together. The real nature of man will be clearly manifest to everyone at the end of history. But meanwhile we need many cultures if we are to grasp the clues to the ultimate nature of man.

It is interesting to consider this from a secular perspective. Suppose one thinks of the dispersal of human beings as coming about, indeed, through the acquisition of reason and language. The Fall, after all, is supposed to have come about through the eating of fruit from the tree of the knowledge of good and evil. At the point at which man can reason things out for himself and, above all, at the point at which man can use language to represent alternatives in the real world, he becomes responsible for himself. He is no longer like the wolf or the cougar who behave simply according to their natures, who have no real choice in the matter, and who are not to be blamed, therefore, for eating the sheep.

Once man has a choice, however, he faces alternatives. The possibility of separation sets in. Men forge their meanings in relatively small groups. One must choose amongst the meanings one has and learn to construct others from them. It is not as if each person pre-existed with all the choices open to him. From this perspective of isolation — certainly a 'fall' from the natural community of the animals — the unhappy tendency is to regard knowledge itself as something which each person possesses in isolation.

Yet we have also seen that there is a tendency for meaning to expand, to become generalized and, in the process, for the principles of reason itself to begin to emerge. The secular equivalent of the incarnation, the point at which men are called back together again, is the point at which this discovery of the principles becomes a real possibility at some point in space and time. As a Christian, Lachance sees this as emerging at a particular point in history — the point at which the meaning of the whole is sufficiently disclosed to us so that we can at least begin to participate in it, even if we cannot completely understand it.

In *The State in Peace and War*, John Watson confronts similar problems. The Hegelian synthesis had emphasized human diversity, but also the rather drastic way which the Absolute might have with that diversity. Generally, the British idealists (with some exceptions like Edward Caird who particularly influenced Watson) had played down the latter aspect of Hegel. They often chose to ignore or denigrate history. But the First World War made it seem all too likely that Hegel was right.

The 'historicist' version of Hegel's theory (the version that greatly influenced Marx) led to the view that people are creatures of the historical processes in which their societies are immersed and lack, for the most part, the power to break free. If one thinks of those 'inevitable' historical processes as manifesting themselves in the modern nation state, one gets a violent kind of nationalism which bears its share of the responsibility for the disasters of our time. Watson thought Hegel's theory could be supplemented to provide a controlled nationalism. Lachance equally sought, in a base which was Thomist and Christian, a modified nationalism.

The other extreme, of course, is the thesis which has its roots in the writings of Thomas Hobbes. Hobbes saw men as essentially self-contained individuals — matter in motion — and as embroiled in a war of all against all. Society is the product of prudence which gives rise to a contract under which men surrender some of their "natural rights" (their right to eliminate others at will, for example) in exchange for peace. In the Hobbesian scheme, the search is for power. Everyone seeks to dominate everyone else. Given the nature of man, a very powerful state — a state exemplified in the person of an absolute monarch — is the only solution and men will prudently contract for such a state of affairs.

John Locke, another Englishman, who himself fled to Holland at one point to evade the wrath of political authority, modified the scheme. In Locke's account of the matter, men seek not so much power as property. A man is less likely to try to eliminate his neighbours than to try to get a high price for his old horse and his rickety carriage. But Locke's people were still individuals conceived as existing independently of society, and society was conceived as a creation of those individuals. Locke, indeed, was the intellectual father of the United States. When Thomas Jefferson and his friends wrote the Declaration of Independence, they took Locke's phrase "life, liberty and property" and, beginning the central tradition of American political compromise, substituted "life, liberty and the pursuit of happiness."

These schemes can also lead to a rather nasty kind of nationalism: the contracting parties owe a debt to each other. In Locke's society, one owes a debt to those who help one to create and keep one's property, and a debt to the community which has an ultimate claim on the natural resources. But one need owe nothing to those outside the community.

In trying to steer between these historic alternatives, the Canadians Lachance and Watson sought a modified nationalism. On both theories the community is mediated by reason and becomes distinct from other communities through shared meanings, but retains its obligation to other communities on account of the common reason which runs through all human activities. For Lachance, this larger bond is strengthened by the fact that all men feel the pull of the call to return to God — even though they may feel it in very different ways in their very different circumstances. In secular terms, again, this pull of the transcendent is essentially the need for a complete system in which the world will finally become intelligible. In Watson's philosophy, God plays exactly this role. For Watson reason constantly seeks to escape from the bounds of any system which encompasses it. Thus there is a demand for a new kind of nationalism, a new kind which might actually safeguard cultural pluralism and permit mutual accommodations amongst peoples. It is important to bear this in mind even while reminding oneself that Lachance was interested above all in the Francophone culture of Quebec and its associated nationalism in Canada.

Both philosophers equally sought to combat what C.B. MacPherson has called the "theory of possessive individualism." Lachance made no bones about his feelings. The doctrine which he called "liberalism" fails finally because it inverts the basic order of values. He spoke gloomily, like Plato, of a general regression since the Renaissance from the objective to the subjective. He thought extreme individualism involved a conceptual mistake which would make law itself impossible: the person is one term in a relation and that relation is social. Extreme individualism makes of law something which stems from the powers of the individual, while in reality it is the law that confers power.

His concern was that the individualist inversion of values would lead to a choice between anarchy and tyranny. If we were to reach the limits of legal subjectivism then, as Plato said, democracy would be the tyranny of the strongest group. Failing that, there would be anarchy. The creation of personal power without responsibility would lead to tyranny.

There is a possibility of mediation only because there is a common good. Lachance evidently conceived this in two ways, one of which stemmed directly from St Thomas Aquinas, and one which did not. He argued in the usual way that there is a common human nature and that what is not natural is destructive. The bases for this notion of a common human nature in St Thomas include the common relation of men to God, the development of rationality as a natural end of man, and perhaps the notion of the agent intellect, the common light as Thomas puts it, which illumines us all. Lachance supplemented the case with arguments about the nature of law. If it is law which gives us power and makes possible the complexity of society, then there must be a common agreement on the desirability of law as a way of doing social business. Above all, on Lachance's theory, law is not a form of force. Within it, the individual finds his power and his freedom.

Thus freedom cannot be the final goal. The goal is, indeed, the proper individuation of human beings. Only responsibility implies liberty. Lachance brings this home forcefully at the end of the book when he is concerned with the problems of international law. One is entitled to liberty because one has responsibilities. Thus the responsibilities determine the powers. It is law which is supreme, a law which derives its force from the ideal of community and not from the arbitrary decision of any individual. Such a law is not destructive of liberty, but is the condition of liberty. The kind of anarchy which implies lawlessness would in fact be destructive of liberty because it does not vest the individual with legal power.

For his part, Watson constantly makes the point that community comes before individuality, that social demands make possible social differentiation, and that liberty follows from responsibility. The Queen's University professor provides an alternative to two doctrines common to the idealists of his time. On the one side, there was the theory which derives from certain readings of Hegel, which holds that what is ultimately real is simply the "absolute mind" — the reality of which distinct individuals are simply an appearance. This view, of course, tends to idealize the collectivity and tends to increase the likelihood that individuals will be swept aside in the name of progress or whatever god happens to reign amongst us. Watson also tries to go beyond the view held by the great American idealist, Josiah Royce, that we should replace the Hegelian idea of the Absolute by the idea of a community of knowers, held together, in the end, by the common features of their knowledge and understanding and feelings about the world. Watson's view seems to be that the common mind develops through a process in which individuals are differentiated from each other. A complex society parcels out duties and opportunities but it also creates religion, literature, and public institutions through which the individuals may come to share each other's activities and experiences.

Individuals must be knit back together again by common ideals and beliefs. There is, underlying it all, a real rational order in the world and human beings seek to find this order. But the order itself is not (as Hegel has often been read as thinking) something which absorbs the individuals. We must find the possibility of a community which expresses all the individuality through a new unity. Watson had spent years reading and commenting upon Imannuel Kant, and his ultimate idea of the unity of men is close to Kant's notion of a kingdom of ends — an ideal society in which the members do not use each other as means to further their own ends but recognize the unique and necessary contribution of each individual and, indeed, are held together by that recognition of uniqueness. In principle, of course, such a 'kingdom' might include all human beings. But its possibility depends on the recognition of shared meanings: there is a culture at its base. There are many ways in which such meanings can be constructed and Kant himself recognized the inevitable plurality of cultures.

Thus Watson searches for a community of experience which contains the materials for individuation. He and Lachance are not far apart. They have, however, opposite problems: Lachance, working from the notion of men as ultimately discrete substances joined together by a common providence, struggles always to make clear the common nature of human destiny. For him, it is the common good, the good which comes from the common human

Je crois...

Public Archives (C87530)   Director of Public Information, World War II

In both English and French Canada, the philosophers — Watson and Lachance, Blewett and Pâquet — agreed that only belief in a Christian universe could finally guarantee human dignity. But the wartime artist unconsciously made a more subtle point: The tentacles of the Swastika might even entangle the cross.

nature, which must unite men. Watson, more insistent on the struggle for individuation — something which has to be achieved in a social process — is at pains to provide a notion of a society in which ultimately there are individuals. Watson and Lachance agree, however, that individualism will produce a society in which unity is possible only in terms of a lowest common denominator — and that common denominator will feed upon greed, possessiveness and the triumph of sensation over reason.

In English Canada and more recently in Quebec, Thomism is frequently regarded as a source of tyranny and oppression, as the backing of an authoritarian church against the real political aspirations of the people. Thomists in Quebec and positivists in English Canada have tended to regard Hegelianism in much the same way. But Hegelian Watson and Thomist Lachance were both concerned to battle tyranny. Both are quite clear about the limits of the authority of church and state.

Both Watson and Lachance were committed to the notion that men cannot in a single lifetime remake their societies *ex nihilo*. They accepted what George Brett, writing in Toronto at about the same time, called the "trite commonplace" that societies evolve and are not simply made. Civilizing depends upon an accumulation of experience which is not possible within a single lifetime and on the creation of institutions which are so complex that they cannot all be kept in consciousness at a single time.

Both writers generally (but not in all circumstances) oppose violent change and disclaim knowledge of any single formula which would solve all the great problems of the hour. One should notice that, in taking this position, they stand squarely against the three political philosophies most popular amongst academics in our own time. They oppose the Lockean social contract theory revived in the United States by liberal philosophers like John Rawls. They also oppose the Hobbesian doctrine revived at Harvard by Robert Nozick, the theory that overriding everything are the simple natural rights of individuals who need have no ultimate social concern for each other. But they also oppose the Marxist position that one can settle the question of right social organization simply by looking at history and finding out the working of the appropriate historical laws. For Lachance there is at least one great break in human history, initiated by God. For Watson, history can be made to part from its path by the understanding of individuals in a real community.

Such theories imply an element of caution. Watson opposed the wholesale transformation of society in a single massive and concerted effort of the kind often proposed by socialists in his own day. We learn slowly over time and in history. We did not and could not remake our society from an empty beginning. Watson also argued that our present experience of bureaucracy should make us leary of such concentrations of power. In these ways, in fact, he resisted the logical thrust toward socialism which his theory would seem to demand, and tried to justify a more conservative position than logic suggested. He did not develop an adequate theory of social institutions, but he does not think any institution should become dominant. Lachance similarly argues for the necessity of a complex division of responsibilities amongst state, church, and family which makes impossible a single over-riding solution.

There is another rather conservative element in these theories. Both Watson and Lachance maintain that there are known and established values that are to be protected. Watson does so because he believes in the logical primacy of the concept of community over the concept of individual and because he believes that the progress of humanity depends upon the ultimate unfolding of the Absolute. He denies that one can be "allowed to do *anything* that one would like to do." Freedom is something we value because we suppose that men set free are capable of good. If we agreed with Hobbes that men, in their natural state, were likely to destroy one another, we would have a different view. Accordingly, Watson says that freedom is good or bad according as the things which can be done with it are good or bad. Furthermore, it is clear, if community is essential for individuality, that there are some things we can only do together. Lachance thinks that there are basic social values which cannot legitimately be eroded by individual action and also that there are transcendent values which have to do with one's prospective salvation. Neither individual nor state may be permitted to act in ways which render more probable the damnation of another.

Indeed society, like the Church, is for Lachance more protector than originator. The task is to conserve and make relevant knowledge which already exists. Watson sees society as involved in a process of change toward the Absolute, but the sense one gets from *The State in Peace and War* is that the more important discoveries have already been made and are generally known to Queens' men.

But though this conservative element occasionally predominates, it is kept in check by the conviction, again shared by both men, that there is much injustice. The world must change and both Watson and Lachance insist that a wide region of power and responsibility must properly be given to individuals in a way which will make social change more likely, and more to the liking of individuals. The question is whether each of them is involved in a conflict which might end in contradiction, and how they regard it as soluble. On the face of it, the necessary grant of freedom to individuals would appear to result in a loss of control which must put at risk the tradition which Watson and Lachance seek to defend. Faced with this problem, each of them settles for the doctrine which Watson calls "Relative Sovereignty." Each of them agrees that spheres must be demarcated within which the individual is unquestionably sovereign, and others within which institutions are finally sovereign.

But what is the principle of this determination? In *The State in Peace and War*, the principle is not entirely clear; it can perhaps best be understood as a series of orders of reflection. For instance, Watson says that the state is a moral agent, though not "directly" so. "The state cannot directly promote morality." If an issue involves a specific act, a choice of what to do here and now, without making up some new rule, it belongs to some individual. The existing rules, for instance, allow us to decide whether to start a widget factory or stay home and go to bed. And, presumably, they are sufficient to cope with the consequences of my choice from the perspective of society. The rules governing corporations, public safety, hours of work and so forth are imagined to be sufficient to deal with whatever results from my decision to make widgets, unless I introduce some new factor with which society has not in the past had to cope. Similarly, the public welfare laws will deal with whatever social problem might result for me or my family from my decision to stay home in bed.

But if the action requires deciding on a new rule we must ask whether or not the proposed rule has validity beyond my immediate act. Generally it does, for the established rules about fairness will usually result in the supposition that what I do can be done by others also. So if my widget factory turns out to be likely to create a new pollutant, I shall need a rule about how such pollutants are to be controlled, and society will have to step in to make that rule. In general, rules are not needed at all unless the action is of such a kind that it will create a precedent for my own future acts or for those of others. If it were really 'completely individual' I should need no rule at all. One does not have to have a rule to sleep in on Sunday morning or to decide whether or not to buy a milkshake.

If the rule does have validity beyond the immediate act, then it involves whatever community might be bound by that rule. If the rule is appropriate to everyone in that circumstance then it belongs to some public institution. If the rule belongs to some subject matter other than rules about rules it belongs to an institution other than the state. For it is generally the function of the state to coordinate the other institutions, to prevent conflict between them, or to make them work more efficiently. The state, of course, may control certain economic institutions or certain educational institutions but it does not, thereby, become an economic or an educational institution. Watson says that the state as we *know* it *consists* itself of institutions and "in truth no institution is sovereign."

In the end, to make these decisions, we must search for the "rational will." The "dissent or assent of individuals does not either prove or disprove its reasonableness," and no serious community is simply concerned with counting heads. Rather, the community must hope that individuals make their decisions on the basis of reason and should not be satisfied until it is clear that, whatever opinions the citizens hold, they do so for reasons. In fact, of course, all serious societies have constitutional arrangements and political provisions which militate against hasty action even when that action is demanded by a vociferous majority. Even in the British system in which Parliament is supreme, the House of Commons may be slowed by the House of Lords. And both could be stopped by a determined monarch who valued some principle enough to risk the monarchy itself.

For Lachance, the question about how one divides up the responsibilities is essentially one of function and nature. By nature man lies on the edge of the natural and supernatural. His function is associated with that bridge. His competence lies in using reason to determine the best way to achieve his end. To that extent he must be free. The state is an arrangement within the context of that necessity and has no freedom of its own. The state is not, for Lachance, *any* kind of moral agent. But there is a common good which it represents and this, in the end, comes closer than one might think to Watson's position.

The difference between Watson and Lachance seems sharpest if one asks about conflicts between some institutions and the state —whether those be the family or the Church. But in his discussion of nationalism and religion Lachance reaches a compromise position which is not far from that advocated by Watson. Both urge that no institution, finally, has absolute sovereignty, and that only concrete reason in a real case can determine the result, though the result will always be conditioned by two principles which both would accept — the principle of continuity of community (the only principle which could, in Watson's view, justify compulsory military service), and the principle of individual integrity.

We can understand both Watson and Lachance through the common thrust toward the organic society which underlies Canadian social history. But one needs to dig deeper if one is to see how such an argument might bear on the issues which may divide us. Are we really one nation or two, or several? How is one to draw the line and, as one draws that line, how does the relation between culture, community, and nation develop?

Chapter 7

Nation, State, and Moral Principle

*I*n the beginning in Canada there was the kind of hope which accompanied the development of the New World — the hope that man would discover his true relation to nature. Thomas McCulloch, almost the first professional philosopher in Canada, proposed a rural idyll in which sensible men would devote themselves to a suitable mixture of hard work, Bible reading, and tough philosophical thinking.

He set out his views in a series of imaginary reports on rural Nova Scotia which he called the *Stepsure Letters* — a chronicle of the folly of those who seek to avoid hard work and get rich by trade, or to replace sound and reasoned religion with the latest revelations from New York or Glasgow. The idea is that there is a proper relation between man and the land. McCulloch's idyll seems to have been a small community, as close to self-sufficient as possible in everything but ideas.

McCulloch's focus on the rural idyll exactly parallels a concern which one finds very frequently amongst Francophone philosophers in Quebec. As late as 1917 it is repeated, for instance, by Louis-Adolphe Pâquet in an essay written for the three hundredth anniversary of the arrival in Quebec of Louis Hébert, the first settler, entitled "La Terre Canadienne." Alas, however, the matter soon becomes complicated. In the writings of Pâquet and others, there is frequently an elaborate rationale: man, situated between the angels and the animals, has a duty to stay close to nature. But in Pâquet's essay one catches another note: nature transformed, civilized, ordered, is made to exhibit more clearly the divine plan. In the process, those who carry out that plan acquire title to it. There is an insistence on that claim which McCulloch does not find it necessary to make. McCulloch could afford to be concerned only with internal threats to social continuity. Pâquet recalls the experience of those whose culture is French in Canada and searches for a defence. The one which he adopts is a combination of a claim like that of Locke that those who transform the environment may claim it, and the notion that those who play a part in the unfolding of divine providence — in making clear the possibilities for man and the real meaning of nature —thereby acquire a claim to it. Thus he speaks both of "natural value" and of "the cooperation of providence."

In English Canada, too, there were complications: the leap from McCulloch, active around the beginning of the nineteenth century, to his successor, Halifax professor William Lyall, who published his major work in 1855 is almost from one world to another. It was not that Lyall had lived it up in the great centres of the world, while McCulloch lived out his life in Nova Scotia — though, to be sure, Lyall did live for a time in Toronto. Rather, Lyall had absorbed a good deal of St. Augustine, who thought that politics only became necessary when man was ejected from the Garden of Eden. The innocence is gone. The Vandals are always at the gates.

Lyall's outlook was strongly against theories of the social contract like those of Hobbes, Locke and Rousseau. This contractual theory of society can be seen as an exercise of pure reason. It takes human beings as *individuals* and sets out to calculate their interests without regard to tradition, the sense of a shared past, and the feelings that bind men together into families, clans and nations. Against all such notions, Lyall maintains that our strongest clue to the nature of reality is in the emotion of love. It is love which, since it transcends personal interest, and since its demands can be met only by a perfect being, leads us to the idea of God. But it is also love which, since it forces us beyond ourselves, leads us to the community. Such an argument is used against the social contract view that we may pick and choose our own community and determine our companions at will. Love leads beyond us and has no explanation in our own being. We must love our neighbour whether or not we can make a deal with him.

In these theories, the boundaries of community are rather vague. McCulloch's rural community must necessarily be small, for it is his thesis that the creation of institutions which permit a departure from the natural life leads to social instability. A large, complex society must have such institutions. Lyall's social emotions ultimately unite all mankind in the eyes of God but, of course, the force of such emotions diminishes with distance and complexity, so one must again have a relatively small community.

How can one explain the fact that men are divided into states and nations? Surely the social effect of the emotions subjected to adequate reason would be a natural world community, or at least a steady progress toward one? Lyall answers that originally "We were to be more intimately associated with our fellows, to have in every way a greater interest in them." It is natural, he thinks, that we should have ties to our families, for the social emotions involve learning and the application of reason. But, that apart, man is one in principle. What intervened was The Fall. "Had man continued innocent, it is questionable if any other divisions would have taken place ... Unquestionably, the division into nations broke the power of evil, made man more helpless, and threw him upon sympathies more limited in their range."

The state is thus a necessary evil. It has its basis in the propensities which turn men against each other. Its history is not encouraging. Nevertheless, "nation and country appeal to our peculiar love. Patriotism is the consequence ... It is love modified by a cause ..." Patriotism is acceptable: it may be part of the road back to union with God. For it does lead men beyond selfishness, it does raise pointedly the question of the nature of our union with our fellow man. We find Lyall deeply concerned about these questions and also convinced that they do not have answers in reason or even in the correct understanding of the social emotions. These modified emotions — love harnessed to a cause as Lyall puts it — are necessary for social continuity because they transcend not only self-interest but also the present moment.

Lyall had to confront a world more complex than that of his predecessor Thomas McCulloch, but Jacob Gould Schurman, who was born the year before Lyall's major book was published and who was to succeed Lyall at Dalhousie University, confronted a world immeasurably more difficult. He was the first major figure in Canadian philosophy to be born in Canada and his life spanned a period from before the union of Upper and Lower Canada to the middle of the Second World War. As a student, he went from Acadia University to England and Germany. As a professor, he went from Acadia to Dalhousie and on to Cornell. He was to become president of Cornell, chairman of the Philippines Commission, U.S. ambassador to Greece, China, and Germany, and one of those shadowy advisors who form the courts of American presidents.

In the world in which Schurman found himself, the idea of nationality had become both difficult and important. The upsurge of nationalism in the nineteenth century, coupled with the mass movements produced by the industrial revolution, the outward thrust of European — and, despite his frequent objections, of U.S. — imperialism, and the confrontations of historically amorphous

Public Archives (26400)   Printed by Ronalds, 1930

Schurman would have liked this poster from 1930 — and enjoyed the ambiguity. Whatever one does with the "British Preferential Tariff" one opens some doors and closes others. That is what a nation is for. (Schurman himself was always suspicious of what lay behind British doors.)

entities (particularly the Turkish and Austro-Hungarian empires) made the question as difficult to pose as to answer. The question could hardly be tackled outside the context of the historical situations in which it made its appearance. Though Schurman had earlier been laying the philosophical groundwork for his ideas, he developed some of them only in the period just before the First World War and in a little book called *The Balkan Wars*. Much of it deals with Bulgaria where the intellectual culture tended to depend upon its Greek heritage while its politics were dominated by the strength of the Ottoman Empire. Schurman is careful to remark that he writes as "an American" perhaps in case someone should think that the parallel between Bulgaria and its relations to Greek culture and Turkish power may sound suspiciously like Canada with its relations to British culture and American power.

The point Schurman makes in this book is that social theory is a matter of understanding the combination of a social process which is essentially evolutionary, and of moral insights which transcend the immediacies of history. Failure to grasp either is ultimately fatal. Thus one must understand that the case for a Bulgarian nation is not to be found in a simple continuity of culture in the sense of literature, the arts, or even the common tradition of the written language. The dominance of Greek culture would weaken any such claim. It is rather to be found in the shared past of struggles won —and even more of battles lost — of problems confronted, and especially of occasions of cooperation.

People can be joined across barriers of language, Schurman observes, if they participate in a common decision, and may be separated if they do not. He might well have said that Francophone and Anglophone Canadians participated in the decisions precipitated by the American revolution and the rebellions of 1837, though they were separated by the decisions made during the Riel rebellions.

But every social problem has a moral element as well. Schurman chronicles the injustices suffered by Bulgarians under Turkish rule and postulates the Bulgarian state as a feasible institution for the rectification of those injustices.

The foundations of this theory are be found in the principles with which we find him wrestling in his first book, published in London in 1881. He called it *Kantian Ethics and the Ethics of Evolution*. The overall aim of the book is to show that Immanuel Kant's view of morality is inadequate, that the "evolutionary ethics" advocated by Herbert Spencer are substantially worse, but that each does, nevertheless, have something to contribute.

Immanuel Kant had held that morality is essentially a matter of rules. To know what you ought to do, you need to know whether a rule of a certain kind can be generated to cover that action. The essence of such a rule is that it should be universal — it should apply to everyone. If I want to know whether I ought to do something or not, I should ask myself whether I would hold that everyone ought to do that thing. Kant also thought that there were other related tests — chiefly having to do with the question of whether or not a given action is consistent with the dignity of all human beings considered as "ends in themselves" or as "members of the kingdom of ends." Mostly, this amounts to asking whether one's actions treat others as the means to some end of one's own or whether they could be regarded as treating others as ends in themselves.

Kant's ethics has always been recognized as clearly focussing on one of the basic components in morality — the transcendence of individual interest. Schurman maintains, however, that Kant's moral theory is "formal" and "empty" and that, while seeming to be objective it is really subjective. It is formal in that it argues that what matters in determining the moral propositions which one should hold is their logical form — universalizable maxims result in acceptable imperatives. One can guess what is wrong: A maxim like "you ought to give water to thirsty dogs" seems clearly "universalizable." But there is always some possible factual state of affairs which would nullify it: suppose the veterinarian has just given Fido some medicine which, if mixed with too much water, simply won't work and Fido will die.

Schurman, in this book and in one a few years later entitled *The Ethical Import of Darwinism* accuses Kant of forgetting when he writes about pure practical reason (the theory of conduct) the essence of Kant's own position about pure reason (reason in its theoretical guise, the kind of thing which we find most often in mathematics). Kant had urged that pure reason, uninformed by experience, could produce defenses for any proposition whatever: indeed, that in certain basic cases, if left to itself, pure reason generates "antinomies," pairs of contradictory propositions which seem equally true. Schurman thought that practical reason uninformed by experience would generate moral nonsense in just the same way. All sorts of principles may be embodied in a given set of events. The context invariably makes a difference. An act done this weekend in downtown Halifax may strongly resemble one done forty years ago in the centre of Hamburg. But one act is a murder, while the other many would judge a brave and praiseworthy act. In one case, it is a policeman on his beat who is struck down with a lead-loaded stick; in the other, it was a Nazi S.S. officer. Thus we might well be able to universalize contradictory maxims if we chose the context carefully enough.

Two basic principles are involved here. One is that people should seek to apply and to accept as decisive the most general and fundamental moral principle which applies to a given situation. The other is that people should seek to apply whatever principle will lead over time to a world in which the most fundamental moral principles can be understood and acted upon. For example, the principle that human life ought to be protected is more general and more fundamental than almost any other moral principle. If you are not alive, you cannot apply *any* moral principles (that makes it fundamental), and all moral agents equally have a concern about their lives (that makes it perfectly general). However, a Bulgarian of about 1910 who discovered two Turkish soldiers with a machine gun and with their backs to him about to shoot some Bulgarian hostages, would have a choice between killing the two of them (if he could) or losing the lives of the hostages. Since the most general principle — to safeguard human lives is not applicable in this case, he might have to choose some lesser principle — to protect the lives of nationalists against members of invading armies. But in choosing a less fundamental and general principle he acquires the obligation to try to create a situation in which those choices are not necessary — to fight for a society in which human life is secure.

Thus we must ask about the community within which one poses these questions. The state, according to Schurman, is the arena in which morality is "objectively realized." In fact he does not seem to mean the state as a political institution which co-ordinates others, but the nation — the moral structure of the community. The nation *is* the arena because it is the largest context of relevance for the determination of the correct maxim. If my family makes me tell lies, I might appeal to some larger community. But the person living in Bulgaria under the Turks is unable to appeal beyond that community with any effect.

Again, two sorts of considerations are involved here. One has to do simply with the facts of power: it is odd for someone in Moscow to do what he thinks right in the belief that his community of relevance also includes Ames, Iowa; for it is unlikely that the citizens of Ames, Iowa will be able to make themselves felt. In Canada, however, the Supreme Court of Canada did (eventually) make it reasonable for those who lived in Quebec under Maurice Duplessis to include the inhabitants of New Westminster, B.C. in their community of relevance when they were protesting against the lack of religious freedom.

But there is a second, much deeper principle involved — the idea of a community of understanding. Moral principles are relevant only where they can be understood. Some human acts are immoral if they are understood against the background of the germ theory of disease, but not otherwise. Some acts are properly judged benevolent by those whose prospective acts are backed by an adequate knowledge and experience of brain surgery but not by those whose acts are not. Thus there must be common understandings and also a common pool of knowledge.

Schurman hoped to show that Kant was right about important aspects of the problem, but that the evolutionists were also right in thinking that time and place made a difference, though wrong in thinking that morality amounted to something like the survival of the fittest. Thus he postulates a community as necessary for the understanding of the intersection of these two concerns. His aim is to show that, though Kant is wrong, it would be more absurd by far to fall into the hands of the social evolutionists. Kant forgets that the concrete content makes a profound difference and, therefore, thinks of all moral principles as relevant to all states of development. But the evolutionists confuse development in time with progress. They confuse a set of facts which is essentially value-neutral with a progression of values.

One can tell what principles are relevant by an analysis of the conflicts which the situation generates. Thus when truth leads to loss of life, it is clear that the situation is one in which, since maintaining life is more fundamental to the continuation of the moral process than telling the truth, maintaining life should have precedence. That principle is also more general — truth telling cannot always be demanded of all agents; the confused, the fearful, and the sick may sometimes be beyond its range. The principle of respect for life is, whatever its limitations, surely wider in reasonable application.

To some extent, these rules will enable us to distinguish between communities. The inability to instantiate certain principles might provide a basis for demands for social reform. We cannot have continuous, intelligible communities without establishing appropriate principles.

The Americans learned that the principles of orderly self government, limited as they were, which normally held in Cook County, Illinois could not be applied in Saigon and we are able to understand something about how we regard ourselves as Canadians by noticing that some moral principles said to be common amongst politicians in Cook County, Illinois, are not acceptable in Carleton County, Ontario. But, of course, the inhabitants of Ottawa form a community which embodies some principles also found in Missoula, Montana, but seemingly unknown in certain political circles in British Columbia.

We must therefore try to see what additional conditions Schurman would want to impose. His formal philosophizing was virtually all done before he became president of Cornell University and the ideas which he had begun to develop in middle life were never completely worked out.

In 1889, Schurman wrote for a magazine called *The Forum* an article entitled "The Manifest Destiny of Canada" in which he emphasized the ability of Canada to unify disparate populations with a constitution which he saw as significantly more flexible than its American counterpart. He also spoke feelingly of the continuity of Canadian history with that of western civilization and (oddly) of our stimulating climate. Nor did he think Canadians would decide to wind up the family business: when people have once made up their minds about something so fundamental as the choice of basic constitutional arrangements for a country, he said, those decisions are not lightly undone. He specifically attacked American proposals for the incorporation of Canada into the U.S.

The theoretical core of his position seems to be that Canada instantiates more perfectly "the federal principle." This does not necessarily help. For "the federal principle" may surely unite communities for which different moral principles are relevant at a given time. But what concerns Schurman is that, in every society which is imperfect but inhabited by at least some rational men, there will be a tension between perceived moral principle and the social order. The ability to cope with this tension is a crucial condition of social continuity and the provision of a forum for appropriate conciliation and reconciliation is therefore a central condition for the creation of an acceptable community. Groups of men whose principles have *enough in common* will, on that view, be better off in such a federation than as independent communities, because the federal principle, if it is to survive, will compel the creation of institutions of a kind which Schurman thinks will lead to genuine moral progress as well. Canada, he seems to have thought in 1889, represented a good balance of common interests, healthy tensions, and flexible institutions.

Schurman had recently left Canada himself. He seems to have gone to Ithaca, New York because it appeared to him that Cornell

University was genuinely more likely than Dalhousie to develop into an institution which would serve the whole community rather than a privileged few. As Schurman became increasingly involved in practical politics, his interest in the possibilities of different kinds of federal union certainly grew. So, in this period, did his associations with the U.S. Republican Party and, more especially, with a kind of conservatism which marked him off from progressive politicians even within that party. He was a long way from Theodore Roosevelt. It is somewhat puzzling now to read his views on trust-busting, the regulation of railroads and other matters having to do with the taming of American capitalism. He had become more interested in the state as conciliator and less convinced, in general, that it *itself* could embody moral principles. These, he increasingly thought, were the affair of the individuals who made up society.

There may also have been changes in his view of Canada. In an address to students in 1896 at the time of a Venezuelan boundary crisis, he is reported to have said that when Canada finally won its independence, Canadians would seek entry into "the American Union." Whether "the American Union" was the Pan-American Union, officially created at the Washington conferences of 1889-90, a project of interest to Schurman, and an organization which Canada resolutely refused to join, or whether the "American Union" was the United States is uncertain. Schurman would certainly have urged some reaching out beyond the limits of the nation state. The occasion of his speech concerned a dispute between Venezuela and the British (over British Guyana), and Schurman, not without reason, may have supposed that Canadian reluctance to join that predecessor to the modern Organization of American States stemmed from the British connection.

Shortly afterwards, however, the United States ended the Spanish-American War in possession of the Philippine Islands and Schurman became chairman of the Philippines Commission. The problem was difficult. The inhabitants were divided by race, religion, custom and political ambition. There was no Philippine nation. At the same time, Schurman and others did not believe that the United States should become a colonial power. He proposed a large measure of self-government (calling on the Canadian experience as evidence that disparate peoples could be united), and a rapid transfer of power to the local authorities. He lost. The United States became a colonial power and Schurman spent the next forty years stumping the country in favour of Philippine independence.

In the end Schurman was driven back to *some* notion of cultural unity, and it is this which he tries to specify as shared experience when he talks of nationhood in *The Balkan Wars*. This is a period in his thought when, frustrated perhaps by his Philippine experiences and clearly aware as U.S. ambassador to Greece of the explosive potential of the Balkans, he comes down outright in favour of nationalism. At the end of *The Balkan Wars*, he writes, "I sympathize with the aspirations of all struggling nationalities to be free and independent."

Evidently, *The Balkan Wars* was an attempt to work some of this commitment out in a concrete situation. *Simple* cultural unity, he decided, is neither possible nor necessary. There are cases like Bulgaria where the literary culture was at that time largely Greek, and where the rest of the culture was certainly complex but seemed to form the basis for a nation and to perform moral functions (the rectification of various injustices) which would not be performed if Bulgaria were part of Turkey or part of Greece. It is here that Schurman calls on the notion of shared experiences of success or failure in the confrontation of moral issues. There is, in short, a Bulgarian cause, which can be traced (and which Schurman does trace) through Balkan history, and there will be disadvantaged classes if that cause is lost to Turk or Greek.

Thus a measure of shared memory of moral responsibility for major events tends to supplement the notions of common principle and of effective mechanism for easing moral tension. Schurman finds these more important than the now conventional notions of common language and folkways — though language and folkways are not unimportant either.

It requires little thought to see that Schurman's theory, too, may generate puzzles. Canadian history is marked by common experiences which result from the fact that both the French who came to Quebec and the highland Scots, for instance, were generally untouched by enlightenment individualism and so tended to reject the social contract thesis of the American revolution. The resulting experience of building alternative institutions is shared by French- and English-speaking Canadians alike. But although our reaction to the First World War gave us an experience unlike that of our American neighbours, it also divided us internally, and tended to separate French-speaking from English-speaking Canadians. Our common experience in combatting the depression of the nineteen-thirties may have strengthened the bonds between the same two groups; but that was an experience which we shared with the Americans as well. The resultant understanding of economic reality

Between McCulloch's rural idyll and Schurman's modern state lay the railroad. But nature is still the master and even the Trans-Canada Limited had to turn aside and carefully thread its way west.

also produced policies and programmes which, to some extent, we shared with the United States.

Schurman would claim that we could decide between the options according to intelligible principles which would have a strong likelihood of deciding the questions. It might be that, after their application, we would be faced with a decision not constrained by the principles but, if so, it would be because the options were all morally acceptable and politically feasible. The crucial questions would have to be: will the new arrangements make it possible to recognize and instantiate more general and more fundamental moral principles than the old? Will they create a political framework capable of more flexibility, speedier adjustment of tensions, and a more open society? And will the new framework organize shared experience into a more coherent and intelligible whole?

Schurman's views come out of his own background as a man of Dutch descent in Prince Edward Island, as a Baptist who studied and taught at Acadia University in a time when higher education itself was thought to be concerned mainly with the inculcation of right principles of action, and who became an important public figure in the United States at a time when the way in which Americans viewed their place in the world was undergoing quite rapid and violent change.

It is interesting to notice that, just as we find McCulloch's rural idyll parallelled in the philosophy of French-speaking Canada, so we find parallels of Schurman's wrestling with nationalism in the work of Louis Lachance. The same tension between notions of universality of the moral order and the particularity of the social order animate Lachance's *Nationalisme et religion*. Lachance concludes that nothing short of the nation state can bind men effectively together but that, again, there must always be a constant adjustment between those virtues and the demands of universality. Although their lives overlapped by forty years or so, it is very unlikely that Lachance and Schurman ever met. But the events of the time rendered the closed compartments of their two solitudes a little leaky.

Schurman's theory makes us aware of the moral and social problems which must lie behind any concept of 'nation.' It also makes clearer just why we need such a concept. Yet it is also clear that one will have to seek farther to find the idea of national identity which might function in any given case — and especially in Canada.

Chapter 8

Canada, Philosophy, and the National Identity

*W*hen we speak of "national consciousness" and "national identity," we may have in mind one of two very different things. We may be referring to the states of mind of those who think of themselves as Canadians at those times when they are thinking about what it is to be a Canadian. Or we may be thinking of those ideas which, whether anyone consciously attends to them or not, are dispositional states which large numbers of Canadians have in common and which shape, to one degree or another, our communal life.

It is important to distinguish. For when it is complained that Canadians lack a strong sense of national identity or an effective one, the complainant is usually thinking about national identity in the first sense. And he often thinks that by giving us something clear to think about — a new flag or a more expensive celebration on the first of July or a poem in praise of maple syrup — he will help us to find a national identity.

Yet being Canadian or Greek or Ethiopian is not, except accidentally, a condition of being aware of some particular object or set of objects. True, by psychological conditioning, one could create a continuous state of mind *characterized* by the awareness of suitable objects. Hitler turned much of German public life into a pseudo-Wagnerian saga. He did create such a consciousness and, for a little while, even some philosophers proved the frailty of reason and stirred to the re-awakening of "the great German folk-soul." But while all that had much to do with being a Nazi, it had little to do with being a German. One can scarcely imagine that Leibniz, Kant, Fichte, Hegel, Goethe, Schumann and Beethoven all shared those particular objects of consciousness, though some of them surely did possess curious objects of consciousness.

Similarly, we could dress up in red suits and march up and down the streets singing Mountie songs like Nelson Eddy and Jeanette MacDonald. In an emotional frenzy we might recapture Point

Roberts from the Americans. But though such fantasies are widely thought to be dear to the hearts of English-speaking Canadians, the consciousness we had created would very likely not be one shared by George Grant or Northrop Frye or Marian Engel or Robin Mathews. And one can scarcely imagine a Francophone counterpart.

National consciousness in the second sense is another matter, and in Canada I suggest that it exists and is strongly influential. It is perhaps wise to remind ourselves that we do act as if we had a national identity. Throughout this book, I have talked of the organic society and I have built an account of how it might be understood through the ideas of community which one finds in Murray, Watson, and Lachance, and how its explicit manifestations might give shape to a theory of the nation like that of Schurman.

Such tendencies show themselves in events which their perpetrators themselves might have found odd. I don't think that R.B. Bennett, for instance, had a very clear political theory. It is sometimes argued, indeed, that he had his brother-in-law, W.D. Herridge, borrow a whole new suit of political clothes from Franklin Roosevelt. Certainly, a lot of the time, Bennett thought of himself as the apostle of the kind of free enterprise endorsed by American chambers of commerce. Yet his government played its part in the development of the nationalized railway and the public broadcasting system. And it was within that party that H.H. Stevens was able to mount his massive attack on monopoly capitalism — even if that attack was finally to split the party. Later that same party became the vehicle for the Diefenbaker campaign whose failure provoked George Grant to a (hopefully) premature lament.

However much the Liberals of those days and ours flirted with the laissez-faire notions to which their name refers, they have not been able to escape the same ideas. It is to them that we owe much of the concept of the crown corporation which has played so large a part in our lives, to them that we owe the paternalist civil service which has frequently been our real governor, and to them that we owe the greater part of our social welfare system. Again, though they thought they despised the new welfare state when Bennett proposed it, they quickly found that the demand for at least a minimal sense of collective responsibility was deeply built into Canadians' culture.

That is not to say that we have not had fierce political arguments, infinitely many lapses into individualism, and long flirtations with continentalism. What is interesting is that those lapses, though most often the fruit of *conscious* policy, have always been stopped by a deeper sense of the community's convictions.

One of the most interesting things about our affairs is that the political surface has rarely been decisive. Rarely, in fact, have our politicians even been taken seriously. We have not seen our political system as the Americans do (as a place for heroes) or as the British do (as the natural setting for stylish, witty young men from Eton and Oxford), but as the natural setting for the somewhat dim-witted men one finds in stories by Stephen Leacock — men whose ability to survive has been closely attached to the stickiness of their fingers. We have rarely sought politicians who promised to take the world in their hands. One might argue that Bible Bill Aberhart, Mitch Hepburn, and Maurice Duplessis are aberrations brought on by bad times, boredom, and a rather well-developed sense of the ridiculous. It gives us pleasure to think that our first prime minister was a lush and, though we all admire D'Arcy McGee, what could we have done with him if he had not had the sense to get himself shot? In my childhood, the young did not view the Fathers of Confederation with the awe that American school children feel for the signers of the Declaration of Independence. As I recall, we snickered at their portraits.

The explanation is obvious: if the community is a reality, it need not be brought into being and sustained by exceptional individuals. The common response to events, rather, is the one to be trusted, and exceptional individuals can be sent to the National Research Council or to other places where they can do no harm.

That communitarianism and its outcomes is one of the sets of ideas which tends to shape our responses. The next most important set of ideas has to do with pluralism. Just as it has rarely seemed sensible to Canadians to suppose that the community is a mere aggregate of individuals, so it has never, I think, seemed even conceivable that we might form a single community.

It is not that we have nothing in common. We do have something in common; but what we have in common cannot be expressed through a single community. In fact this pluralism is related to our communitarianism. If one thinks of a community as a contrivance of its individual members, something which can be made and un-made at will, then one can readily think of a community as large or as small as one pleases, and as having the capacity to include within itself any amount of diversity which can be spanned by political compromise. Americans have had increasing doubts, but, traditionally, they saw a society which might encompass the whole of their geographical area and which, in principle, might spread and encompass the world. If one thinks, instead, of a community as something which has its own structure and its own kind of continuity, something within which we are individuated, then it must embrace a kind of unity which may limit both scope and variety.

We need to admit that this rather clannish notion produces problems. Despite our pious pretensions, we did not establish a society which could accommodate Louis Riel, many of the indigenous societies, or the special communalism of the Doukhobors. It is possible that this is so because we have had, at every level, to contend with incompatible ideas.

Our existing political institutions are borrowed. In 1867, we attempted to replace our essentially British political forms with a compromise between them and American federalism. In the process, though we provided fairly well for individual rights, we provided very badly for group rights. We knew that we needed them. A communitarian society must have them — for it is composed of real communities within which the important life goes on. Vestigial group rights having to do with language in the federal and Quebec legislatures and with denominational schools were entrenched in the British North America Act; but they proved too feeble even to guarantee that one of the local school systems in Ottawa should remain Francophone as well as Catholic.

With communitarianism and pluralism goes a third set of fundamental ideas which cluster around our sense of history. If one thinks of communities as natural phenomena within which individuals develop, rather than as simple creations of ready-made individuals, one must be interested in history. Less obviously but equally importantly, pluralism and an interest in history go together. A simple slice of the present will not distinguish between momentary groupings and those which are deeply woven into our national life.

History has been something at which we have excelled and which we have used to make our points to one another. The list of historians whose names are known to most literate Canadians is surprisingly long: Creighton, Lower, Morton, Berger, Garneau, Groulx, Bergeron, Ouellet ... But we have also had more than our evident share of theoreticians, philosophers of history and philosophers for whom history was a central notion. Amongst the professional philosophers of our past that list, again, is long: some, like George Brett, set out deliberately to be historians of philosophy and saw philosophy as an historical discipline. Others like William

Lyall, John Clark Murray, George Blewett and Rupert Lodge —the backbone of philosophy in English Canada — did not think of themselves as historians but nonetheless held that philosophy can only be understood as a developing historical process.

Our theory of history, however, has run well beyond the formal confines of academic history and philosophy. It is not accidental that in English-speaking Canada our foremost literary critic, Northrop Frye, is chiefly famous for a theory of the history of literature, or that our greatest economist, Harold Innis, cast his work in the form of a theory of history.

In philosophy today the tradition continues. The Canadian philosopher best known to the Canadian public, at least in English Canada, is certainly George Grant whose work has always been cast in an historical mold. And the philosopher best known to English-speaking philosophers outside Canada is William Dray, whose work, though very different in character, is also devoted to the philosophy of history. In many ways, no two philosophers are so unlike as Grant and Dray. Grant's rather apocalyptic vision of our national downfall and his unending quest for being — a quest which has taken him through the philosophies of Plato, Hegel, Simone Weil and Heidegger — contrast sharply with Dray's lifelong search for clarity and precision about the elements of the problem of historical explanation. Yet there is a connection. Both Grant and Dray have insisted that there is a perspective which belongs to the humanities, and that accounts of human affairs are not simply to be reduced to the law-like causal models of physics. Both have insisted that such a perspective is rooted in an understanding of history. Grant and the late Donald Creighton have often shared the same High Tory outlook on Canadian history, but it was to Dray that Creighton turned when he sought to exemplify the kind of philosophical commitment which he found in his own historical methodology.

History is equally central to thought in French Canada. Nationalists like Lionel Groulx have quite naturally tended to make their case in historical terms, and history has been a central focus of their debate. Traditionalïsts like Mgr Pâquet also appeal to history. Louis Lachance did not simply recapitulate the thought of St. Thomas, but added his perspective on history.

But one must see these central notions against something which has had a profound impact on our history — the crisis of knowledge.

West of Thunder Bay and north of the Lakes, Canada is the creation of technology. The railway determined the shape of prairie

THIS IS NO TIME FOR PARTY

VOTE · UNION · GOVERNMENT

Is it ever a time for party? George Grant saw Canada as ultimately shaped by a destiny which politicians could not control. Here, the politician seems, whatever the intention, a little reluctant to go along with destiny.

settlement, the industrialization of central Canada, even the form of religion. One could farm only where one could ship. Trains full of grain one way could not run empty the other way. The specifications for parts of the Grand Trunk Pacific provided for different grade limits, east and west bound, nailing some of our economic and political arrangements literally into the ground. Towns were located to fuel and water the trains and were necessarily too small to accommodate all the religious sects, forcing de facto unions and paving the way for the United Church.

But our knowledge has failed us repeatedly. Our know-how created a technology which forced settlement patterns certain to bring about a final clash with the followers of Louis Riel, but offered nothing by which to settle such a dispute. The resultant tragedy is still central to the feelings in French Canada about the runaway technological civilization of English Canada.

Technology, in due course, turned on the victors in that campaign. Large scale, intensified, mechanized farming was necessary to support the railway. Gluts of grain and a spreading dustbowl were the result in the 1930s. The West has been saved in large measure by the demand for oil and potash; but technology will take away what it has given and the development of a balanced economy in the West is still circumscribed by a railway system which cannot quite cope with the wheat.

Canadians understood all too well how the economic devastation of the 'thirties was related to the Second World War. The sense of helplessness which those events engendered left deep scars, and when, after the war, we came to understand that the technology which had won it for us could also destroy us we became, I think, subtly different — more concerned with the short range, less with ultimate things.

The Second World War left Americans — or at least their political leaders — with a sense that they had entered the world decisively, achieved their goals and could cope with the result. It more often turned Europeans inward in search of new understandings. American thought ran to behaviourism, decision theory, logical analysis and new and tougher kinds of logical pragmatism, while European thought led increasingly to phenomenology, existentialism, and to progammes which emphasized the inner life and the increase of understanding.

Canadians had been more directly exposed to the impact of technology on history. We tended not to feel the immediate post-war euphoria or the subsequent paranoia which gripped Americans when they found that they had not really chosen their part and could not write the next act. Equally, however, we lacked the tradition which allowed Europeans to turn inward.

The result seems to have been a kind of passivity. English and French Canada drifted into new forms of an old collision. Many regions accepted chronic unemployment while others accepted an economy dictated by the convenience of foreign corporations. Our postwar foreign policy is memorable only for our recollections of Lester Pearson's bow tie. We turned to little things which we could achieve — small-scale ameliorating social services, or the removal of the worst stupidities in our legal system.

Our knowledge dictated our ways of dealing with nature and with each other, and created a system within which we became increasingly passive for lack, or so we might have imagined, of any other alternative. But there are alternatives, and the philosophical insights we have amassed in the last hundred and fifty years can help to clarify them.

Philosophy has flourished in Canada because we have constantly had to reconcile conflicting intuitions — partly in our own affairs and partly between them and those of the cultures which have surrounded us. Originally, in English Canada, philosophy was stimulated by the need to train clergymen who would have to argue their way in a pluralistic society and who would have to face the nineteenth-century confrontation of science and religion. In French Canada philosophy goes back at least to the first formal disputation on July 2, 1666, and was a necessary part of a religious life in which the expression of intuition through reason was an established norm.

The founding period of philosophy in English-speaking Canada was the middle of the nineteenth century. A majority of our earlier thinkers were Scots immigrants. William Lyall and Paxton Young began as devotees of the Scots school of 'common sense' philosophy, one of whose tenets was that reason can never wholly replace intuition. But Young became a philosopher in the mold of the British idealists though, indeed, he seems to have developed one of the crucial arguments before the English philosopher T.H. Green. Lyall added Augustinian and Leibnizian strands to his philosophy in a way which gave it a more rationalist cast. Murray *may* have been tending toward Hegelianism before he left Scotland but he certainly developed a firm kind of Hegelian rationalism while he was in Canada. Watson came from Scotland with the idealism of the Cairds as his stock in trade; but he deepened their appreciation of history and gradually developed a theory of public experience which contrasts sharply with the notions of private experience that tended to be characteristic of the British empiricists and to lurk imperfectly examined in the works of some of the British idealists. Lyall, too, was clearly working toward a theory of experience with different notions of subjectivity and objectivity.

There are thus two fundamental tendencies — one, toward system and rationalism; the other, a search for accounts of experience, in the sense of the experience of a community as opposed to the purely private experience of the Cartesians on the continent and empiricists in Britain.

Cartesianism came to Quebec at the beginning. For Mgr de Laval had been a pupil at Laflèche where Descartes studied. But the tendency from the beginning was to fight the individualist version of Cartesianism in French Canada as well as in English Canada. To know that our philosophers felt a need to fight this battle — even if it has been a failure — tells us much about ourselves.

In the Thomist tradition of French Canada Pâquet insists upon it. From the Hegelianism of English Canada, Watson too insists on the role of reason. If we can see that reason is public, and that since experience has a rational order it is, in one respect at any rate, public, we have made some progress toward overcoming the subjectivist malaise.

But if men are reasonable why do we not at once solve all of our problems? The Hegelian rationalism which became popular in English Canada proposed to answer that question. The suggestion was that reason and experience cannot finally be separated. It is by finding the public order in experience that reason comes to have a subject matter and the possibilities of reason itself become available to us. Thus reason reveals itself in an historical development and not as a *fait accompli* and we must accept that there are different historical strands which cannot be consolidated without loss and distortion. Reason is not to be used as a substitute for force, a way of bringing one's opponent to his knees, but as a device for exploring alternatives and for restraining action based on the full force of this morning's beliefs.

All of the philosophers in this list were communitarians who tried to make intelligible the notion of a community as an historical entity with claims of its own. Murray, Watson and Blewett all held that the individual derives his identity ultimately from the community, that I would not know who I was if I were alone in the universe. Lyall, like Augustine, stressed the importance of love as a hallmark of reality, but it is one which is only possible within a community.

The same period in French Canada saw a consolidation of thought in the Thomist revival. Eclectic manuals of philosophy

Philosophers like Pâquet thought French Canada must stay close to nature and preserve its continuity. But it was to have its place, too, in the universal struggle of humankind. The sunny farmland and the final reminder that one lives "for humanity" suggest that the artist may have understood that not everyone would want to join the 178th battalion.

which used ideas of Descartes and Locke, and strands of thought also influenced by the common-sense philosophers, tended to be replaced by philosophies based on the work of St. Thomas Aquinas.

The Thomist philosophy, which had been developed to cope with Arab science and thought in the High Middle Ages, had the obvious attraction of separating faith and reason in a way which promised a minimum of fruitless confrontation. But we have seen that in French Canada it was frequently coupled with a renewed interest in history. In addition, the Thomist doctrines of community were developed by a line of philosophers whose work culminates in the writings of men like Charles de Koninck and Louis Lachance.

Though, to a degree, the Thomism of French Canada and the Hegelianism of English Canada clashed, they did so within a framework of common agreements. Mgr Pâquet attacked Hegelianism on the ground that the social theory of Hegel was cruel. Hegel, he took it, supposed that history justified events and, if so, history justified a long chain of cruel conquests. (We might guess which conquests he had in mind.) Surprisingly, Watson, too, rejected the notion of justification by history on the ground that, though we cannot know what history will reveal to us (including a full understanding of the nature of reason), we can provide for a world in which time is important by creating political institutions which provide for a pluralism necessitated both by our uncertainties and by the fact that not all values can co-exist in a single society.

The Thomists tended to think of the Hegelian idealists as rather given to subjectivism. But in Toronto, George Blewett, perhaps our most distinguished native born philosopher, tried hard to conceptualize clearly the Canadian relation to nature, emphasizing the fragility of the natural environment and its essential independence of us — he even thought the earth had a right to respect for forms of being unlike us. At the same time, he was writing sympathetically on Thomism around the turn of the century — long before Toronto's bright orange had begun to pale.

Lachance, as we saw, may never have spent much time reading Watson, but he comes to a kind of Thomism within which many of Watson's concerns turn out to be recognized. Indeed, the Thomist tradition like the Hegelian tends toward the dissolution of the subject-object dichotomy in the social sphere.

Thus we have the basis of a Canadian world view that emphasizes community, reason, and our collective relation to nature. The alternative view which sees men as individual, experience as immediate and independent of reason, and nature as something mainly to be *used* requires a different view of knowledge.

In the individualist view of the world, knowledge is essentially something which individuals carry around in their heads. Knowledge is relative to the knower and it tends to be concerned with the power to enhance the individual's well being and to transform nature. If one takes the view to which both Canadian Hegelians and Thomists subscribed, knowledge is a property of the community, transmitted by tradition and institutions and shared through the community.

But, history and the Canadian crisis of knowledge put pressure on Hegelian and Thomist alike. In the trenches of the First World War, a disillusioned generation concluded that the community had failed. The march toward unreason cut more quickly into the Hegelian tradition in English Canada than into the Thomist tradition in French Canada. The concern with history continued and was even strengthened by philosophers like George Brett at Toronto. At the University of Manitoba, Rupert Lodge tried to develop a more trenchant critique of claims to knowledge. Across the country one could still find the Hegelians at work — Herbert Stewart at Dalhousie, James Ten Broeke at McMaster, John Macdonald at the University of Alberta. But they produced no new all-embracing system and became guardians of a doctrine which seemed harder and harder to express clearly as time went on.

At Toronto, George Brett produced, in the early years of the century, a massive work which he called the history of psychology. In fact it is largely a history of philosophical theories of a rather special sort, those which have to do with the structures through which men and the world are thought to interact. Brett dominated philosophy at Toronto for the better part of four decades; during which he wrote no further major works but kept up the search for a context within which scientific and technological knowledge could be made to show their real strengths and weaknesses. The enigma of George Brett remains, but, through his cautious writings some features of his philosophy are clear. He thought all kinds of knowledge are misleading apart from their historical context. Our science is the development of a situation which posed particular problems.

Brett was very interested in the relation of technology and knowledge. And this is very important for it gives us our first clue as to how one might identify and try to cope with the crisis of knowledge. The period of the rise of science is also a period in which men found classical skepticism fascinating. Sextus Empiricus was popular amongst thinkers. The hunt was on for a new notion of objectivity. Science provided it in the form of a technology of measurement. But that technology only makes sense in a certain circumstance and against a particular background. Divorced from the context, it becomes something else. If men do not experience uniformly, we can devise machines which do — or seem to — and make them the touchstones of reality.

To understand the limits and self-denying ordinances which we need, we must understand the history of the search for knowledge. But history is a different mode of knowledge. There is a history of the measurable, and, as Brett well knew, a history of measurement. Yet there is no measurement of historical claims. Science both needs history and renders it dubious as a discipline. In our lack of understanding, we are apt to become the victims and not the masters of the development of technology. Hence, perhaps, the crisis of knowledge, and hence (though Brett did not say so) it might be that the crisis is particularly acute in Canada, a country with properties not envisaged in the historical development of our science and technology.

In the same period, Rupert Lodge attempted to create a new theory of the history of philosophy. Philosophy he thought dealt with generalities so universal that they lay beyond the basic assumptions of all other disciplines. Such a stance is necessary to provide a critique of knowledge but is not itself susceptible to criticism. Its systems end in impasse beyond which one cannot reach.

In Toronto, Harold Innis paused in his work on the history of cod fishing (and related matters) to be quoted as having said that philosophy was "dead and stuffed." He had studied philosophy at McMaster under James Ten Broeke, the last perhaps of the great idealists in the Hegelian tradition that we have talked about. But Ten Broeke seemed unlikely to have successors of the same ilk. Innis took himself off to Chicago in search of a value theory in economics and then found himself a post in the University of Toronto's department of political economy where he wrote theoretical history. He has not been alone. I do not know what we should now call theoreticians of the human condition but since then many of our most distinguished ones — George Grant, Northrop Frye, Donald Creighton, Marshall McLuhan and recently Dennis Lee — have been found outside philosophy departments, most of them for the whole of their academic careers. Grant is a philosopher in the obvious sense and one cannot well read Frye without concluding that he knows as much philosophy as most of us. Dennis Lee draws his inspiration from Martin Heidegger.

Innis best illustrates the attempt to find a new base. He wanted knowledge of values, but not the sort of knowledge which contemporary philosophers at Oxford or Cambridge or Harvard (or for that matter Vienna) were apt to give him in the years following World War I. They were teaching the foundations of moral knowledge — how value statements got their meanings, whether value propositions were true or false, how 'right' was related to 'good,' how reason and intuition were related to value claims. Their picture, rather generally, I think, was that the problem of value theory was about how to choose between proffered propositions about values. Innis came to think that our values were apt to be chosen for us in the course of other choices. Communications systems have biases. The fact that it is more efficient for manufactured goods to travel from Toronto to Edmonton than from Edmonton to Toronto or even from Edmonton to Vancouver, structures life in all three cities. The distribution of power and the ways in which men can and must conceive values are thus constricted.

I think that, if one takes this notion seriously, the problem of values is then not how to choose amongst propositions but how to envision social structures within which one or another range of values might arise. One does not question value propositions — for those come with a limited set of options. One asks how to change the options and whether one should change them. One might think that this would leave the traditional philosophical questions substantially unchanged but, in fact, they are changed in important ways: it turns out that what is at stake is our way of envisaging ourselves and our societies. It turns out that the problem of knowledge of values is not primarily one to be decided by examining the conditions and results of introspection or by reference to self-evident premises — the two most common accounts of such matters — but by looking at our ways of systematizing knowledge.

Indeed, what is put in question is the very basis of enlightenment individualism. According to John Locke and David Hume, the two great eighteenth century empiricists with whom G.R.G. Mure associates the rise of capitalism, the best approximation to knowledge (weak though it is) is through the apprehension of sensory data. But if Innis is right, all such data will reveal is the bias of the system in which they occur. Classical empiricism might produce the ultimate degradation in which, in McLuhan's terms, the medium becomes the message.

One of the most common alternatives is some notion that we can substitute for the now suspect individual experience a set of commonly agreed-upon conventions of measurement or just some common way of talking about things. If we reject that, we may be left with only the pragmatic notion that we should do what works or what pleases us. The tendency to rotate freely amongst these options leads to the impasse which Lodge diagnosed.

But we can combine Innis's notion with the older Canadian philosophical traditions we have talked about to see the beginning of a way out. First we would accept that we have to take history seriously.

A claim to knowledge is not based on immediate sensory experience or on some convention of measurement or on some pragmatic notion of the sort to which Richard Nixon said he subscribed. Rather, a claim to knowledge is based on what the community historically had taken to be the tradition to be passed on. To mount a critique, one must wind back through the system and see how the tradition came to develop, what options there were, how standards came into play. A crisis of knowledge is created when the claims to knowledge undermine the community's ability to survive and when the community and its members can no longer find themselves represented in those claims. Thus, for instance, the claim that knowledge reveals the ultimate reality to be a kind of machine monster in which there are only molecules composed of atoms whirling in the void is finally meaningless. The knower has disappeared from the world. No one befriends, marries, grieves for or is cruel to atoms. More to the point of our discussion here, if 'knowledge' reveals that the only possible economic arrangement is one in which individuals must be dehumanized and communities must be torn apart by pitting men against each other, then it cannot be knowledge in the sense of a tradition which a community can accept, build on, reflect on, and continue to create.

Knowledge *per se* does not really consist of sensory impressions, or arbitrary measurements according to devices (like footrules and micrometers) which we invent, or rules of thumb about what works. Knowledge in a society based on capitalist economics and the notion of individuals locked up inside their own heads and busy competing against one another does, no doubt, consist of such things. But, if the system fails to support itself or the individual who 'knows' and the community on whose existence he depends, then it ceases to be feasible in the world. Such a basis of knowledge is clearly inadequate.

It is not that we should not be proud of our science. It is just that we should realize that science is the product of a community. It could not be created out of nothing by one man from his immediate experience or by some group of men arbitrarily agreeing upon the technology of measurement. It can only exist — as historians of science like Thomas Kuhn have recently been at pains to point out — in a community. Knowledge, indeed, reflects as much as it sustains the community which produces it. It is not even the sum of all the things which individuals know but rather the basis on which communities exist. (Our libraries contain many facts which no one at present knows.)

This is the viewpoint that makes philosophers like George Grant both so greatly pessimistic about the possibility of being civilized or even human without those traditions, and so earnest in their pursuit of some deeper being. Now, Grant's despair at the downfall of John Diefenbaker becomes comprehensible: it was not that Diefenbaker was a learned man, or a great 'leader of men,' but that Diefenbaker symbolized the commitment to history.

Our philosophical explorations have revealed the need to take a new look at the ways in which we can conceptualize the community, its organization and its culture.

Part III

Exploring Solutions

Chapter 9

Community, Politics, and Pluralism

*T*here are three well-known theories about the state. On one of them, which we inherit from the Greeks from whom we get the word politics, the state is a mystical union of man and place. On a second, which comes from Hegel and the modern effort to rebuild the social bonds, the state is the source of the ultimate solution to our identity crisis: it is the unity of subject and object and of man and man. On the third which comes, I think, out of Aristotle by way of the mediaeval philosophers, the state is an institution — that institution which coordinates the others.

It seems clear, in Canada, that the mystical union of man and place is not to be had. For men are not barnacles. They attach to places not out of some natural stickiness but by way of a culture. Whether or not we should have several states and whether or not we do have several nations, it is certain that we have several cultures.

The effort to confine them to a place — the French culture to Quebec, the indigenous cultures to a fringe beyond which we happen not to want to push — is an old one. It is sometimes aided and abetted by the friends of those cultures. But it must end in disaster.

If those whose affinity is to the French-Canadian culture are to be confined to Quebec they will eventually go their own way for better or for worse. If the Indian and Inuit cannot make their presence felt in the centre of the country they will eventually perish: for the English and the French cultures loom over them and can be controlled neither by good will nor by the Mounted Police. Trudeau, tinned peas, and television can be contained by no line. If any place stands irrevocably tied to a given culture, it lies outside the bounds of multicultural Canada.

It may engender a patriotism and it is as well that there should be some places which are tied in this way to particular people — some valleys that are home to a very special Québécois culture, a land which Doukhobors will eventually declare home, the traditional lands of the Inuit, the islands which one day (I hope) we will restore to the Haida. But these *places* are *not* the basis of the state. If anything, they provide a good argument for restricting the power of the state.

Nor is it open to us to have the Hegelian state which is concerned, as we have seen, with the loss of identity in the modern world — with the tendency of men to put themselves into a world in which they could not find themselves because their actions had been absorbed into a faceless mass of acts and ideas.

But Hegel noticed that there does exist what he called "objective spirit." In a sense we are all tied together by ideas through which we express ourselves and which also form the basic structures of the social order. Few people have many original ideas. Our ideas are shared and form the basis of a social bond. Yet we feel uneasy because it is the character of those ideas that may swallow us up.

Take the simple notion that men can be individuated by their material possessions — that idea, well enough known to Hegel, is used by every writer of automobile advertising. A man, according to our public teaching, can distinguish himself and come to feel at home in the world by buying the right brand of automobile, wearing the right underwear, and lately by acquiring the right smell. These ideas are widely enough shared, even by people who publicly deny that they share them, to motivate an economy. Hegel's solution was to imagine a society in which the shared ideas were better ones — based not on possession, perhaps, but on brotherhood, concerned not with horsepower, odour and linen but with God, freedom and immortality.

But, though we may share the public ideas in larger measure than we are prepared to admit, there is a logical difficulty. We sense it well enough. We chafe a little uneasily at the public ideas which are given to us, however good they may be. Even if society instantiates all and only ideas which we accept, we know that the bureaucracy and the keepers of public morality are to be resisted just a little. For we know that they work to rules which order things in boxes into none of which any of us quite fits.

The difficulty which we sense comes, after all, from the fact that we are particular. It may be through the public culture that we come to express ourselves. But there can be no question of its succeeding or failing unless there is, after all, something to express.

That something has to be unique. It is what is *expressed through* the general ideas, but, without it, there is nothing to express.

For us in Canada it is not just that there exists this tension, as philosophers would have it, between universal and particular — a tension which Hegel (for all his struggles against it) always tended to resolve on the side of the universal. There is also the fact that it appears to us as the problem of the plurality of cultures.

We know that the human possibilities cannot all be expressed through a single culture. And so we have always opted — against the best advice of Lord Durham and even of John Stuart Mill — to preserve several cultures. If we are unique particulars, then, even though we depend upon cultures for our expression, no single culture — and no possible combination of cultures — can ever exhaust our possibilities.

The society which perfectly expressed all that we had to express, the society to which Hegel looked forward (not as something which would come about tomorrow or next year, but as something that, perhaps inevitably, *would* come about) is not one which we are prepared to accept. Pluralism we have and shall have — or we shall have nothing.

This leaves us with the older idea that the state is what co-ordinates the other institutions. It is at this point that one must clearly distinguish between community, state and nation. The community is what (through culture) legitimizes, gives force and shape, to the institutions. The nation is the principle, embedded, as we saw in Chapter 8, in dispositional ideas, recollected in shared experiences, expressed through moral convictions, which shapes all the institutions. It is for this reason that we may debate in Canada whether we have one nation, or two or several. I incline to the view that we have one for the reasons which I set forth in the three previous chapters — that there are underlying unities in our principles.

But it is debatable. In French Canada, when the dominant institution was the Church, it was natural for thinkers to think of "deux nations." For if anything was Québécois, it was the Church, an institution not French, not American, quite unlike its counterparts in English Canada. It gave shape, furthermore, to two of the three other great institutions. The educational system in which the Québécois participated was almost wholly church-governed. The legal system, Roman and French in origin, took its moral shape from the same source. The economic institutions, though the church influenced the growth of the cooperative movement and the formation of the Catholic trade unions, were essentially neither Québécois nor Canadian.

In those terms one might argue that the central dispositional ideas were Québécois, that the shared remembered experiences were Québécois and that the principles at stake were Québécois. Yet even

Charles de Koninck, who influenced the Tremblay commission, on the whole preferred to talk about "la patrie" and about a real "patriotisme." (The commission also learned a good deal about the complications of the idea of "nation" from J.T. Delos who taught at Laval University and was recognized as one of the world's experts on the subject.) De Koninck saw the federal system as a great protector — *rempart contre le grand état*. He said that the term 'patrie' was preferable to 'nation' because it stood on surer ground —speaking of common origin and commending implicitly the virtue of loyalty which Cicero had recommended so eloquently. Though he noticed that it, too, could be deformed, taking on the character of egoistic individualism which people sometimes attached to nations, it evidently had, for him, a more limited scope and could be tied more firmly to something intelligible.

For to adopt the further term "nation" would be to draw lines against the rest of the country in much firmer terms. Two different communities and cultures can authenticate the same institutions but, if so, those institutions will tend to express themselves as one nation. And it is not part of de Koninck's case to argue that there are no common institutions. Indeed, there *are* common institutions and there *must* be if we are to be protected against "le grand état."

That case has been strengthened since the quiet revolution. For, as the other institutions eased away from the church, they adopted models closer to those which have been common in English Canada. The Quebec universities have the same kind of relation to the state as those in Ontario. The school systems are run on a pattern not unlike that of Ontario or Manitoba. The law, in any case, has had to assimilate much of the English common law. The criminal code we have always had in common, and the civil law has moved of necessity closer to the model in English Canada, despite some anguish on the part of reformers who would like to regain its lost purity.

One must agree that there are several cultures. One must agree that the English and French peoples are distinct and, therefore, that "la patrie" does not have the same sense for each. Patriotism may not, therefore, have the same expression in each culture. But we may, for all that, have one nation. One nation does not entail a monolithic state. The relation of the *nation* to all the institutions makes it clear that the nation is not the state in the sense in which the state is the coordinating structure which keeps the others from colliding. Indeed, it is the force of "la patrie" which may, finally, make us insist that "l'état" is to be guarded *against* as much as used.

To see this, one must distinguish once again, between the state as co-ordinator and the state as controller.

The various institutions — economic, legal, political and educational — each have goals of their own which are rooted in basic human needs. Men need to produce to survive, and to exchange goods and services if they are to rise above the brutes. That order has to be patterned on an idea of justice which, in its natural form, is the idea and ideal of law. Men are born and die, but societies continue. Education provides social continuity, adapts the available talent to the social need, looks beyond the immediate. All social order points to something else — an ideal to which men must stand in some clear relation. There is no easy substitute for economic, legal, political and religious institutions.

The state, by contrast, has no goal of its *own*. The common good, the ideal of justice is not to be found in the political life but in the law. Rather the state must deal with those problems which arise because the existing institutions must cope with outside forces or because they collide in their use of resources, manpower, and ideas. The ideal coordinator is the culture itself — the basic values, beliefs and arts which bind us together and make our lives intelligible.

The only thing which the state can seek on its *own* is power. Everything else which it seeks is, in part at least, the goal of some other institution. If the state supposes that it has an interest of its own and acts on it, then it acts in the search for power. The exercise of political power creates a situation in which one man can determine the actions of another. When this happens, the person ordered ceases to be a functioning moral agent. The person ordering has taken on the moral life of the person ordered. This is an evil not because individualism is a true doctrine but, on the contrary, because it is a false doctrine. To act morally is to transcend one's own interests and act in the interests of all. But one who is deprived of the right to act for himself loses his claim to be part of that collectivity. It is for this reason, I think, that Lord Acton remarked that political power necessarily corrupts. The politician who uses power in this way acts as the civil devil — the swallower of souls in a secular cause.

The state is then left to coordinate, to negotiate, to seek agreement. In a world in which the other institutions functioned perfectly, the state could wither away. Hence Proudhon called himself an anarchist (though he was a mutualist and no individualist); and Marx hoped for the disappearance of the state. It was the state as seeker after power that Lenin denounced as a body of armed men, having in its possession jails. It was this state which Russell denounced in *Power*.

In Canada, there are further complications. The state as power seeker — "le grand état" which de Koninck deplores — imposes order. But a pluralistic community must develop its own order through its own cultures, and ultimately express itself, perhaps, as the nation it is without an order imposed from above.

Though Proudhon has always been kept at arm's length by our thinkers, his spirit has flickered about in the background. Viger alleged that François-Xavier Garneau tried to imitate him; Murray quoted Proudhon (with a note that one should not exaggerate) and preached a cooperative order; Bourassa quoted Proudhon's attack on property. There are echoes of the hope for a cooperative society in the writings of men like Wilfred Keirstead, the New Brunswick philosopher who performed many practical tasks for the provincial government. In our own time, much of the writing of George Woodcock can be seen as a search for the natural community without the state.

To the extent that institutions are imperfect and that there is an outside world, the state must be structured so as to limit its danger and encourage the community to develop from the bottom up and not from the top down. All restrictive constitutions — even bills of rights — are to be regarded with a certain measure of suspicion just because they tend to entrench existing knowledge, class bias and interests. Take, for example, freedom of the press. That freedom may entrench the right of Lord Thompson to own newspapers rather more than it entrenches the right of coal miners on Cape Breton Island to free expression. Freedom of speech may obtain more for those who own large meeting halls than for those who hold forth on the street corner. Entrenched bills of rights have not usually done what was expected of them, because they have been phrased to cast a special advantage — essentially they have been phrased within the confines of a given technology. Thus if one grants freedom of speech without explaining it, one gives the advantage to those who can afford to buy a newspaper, or control a television station.

The right to be heard and the right to know are perhaps the two most fundamental rights in the traditional sense. With them go the right to have as much voice as anyone else in the choice of political arrangements, to come and go in peace, to have one's privacy protected, to be safe from having one's house ransacked by the police or the revenue service without substantial ground, to move around without arbitrary demands to see one's 'papers,' the right to a fair trial and the right to make one's own arrangements with God inside or outside the United Church of Canada. Of these, the right to privacy is the most difficult to provide; but, again, it can be posed largely in terms of a prohibition on the storing and dissemination of unnecessary information, together with the continuous right of access to whatever information *is* stored.

This book, of course, has suggested a cluster of rights of a very different sort, and a very different way of looking at this question. Chiefly it is this: if we all derive our identities from the community and if we all take part in building the community, then we have the right to a share in whatever the community has, up to the point, at least, of being able to carry out our *duties* as citizens. Indeed it is our duties, our *obligations*, which come *first*. It is because I have an obligation as a citizen that I have a right to be heard, a right to know, a right not to be hassled in a way which will keep me from doing my duty. In the same sense, of course, the community cannot have me do my duty — as maker of community and sustainer of the identities of all others — if it starves me to death. Most of all, it must provide me with as much opportunity as anyone else to *contribute* something to the community — it must seek to find for me a real place and a real function.

But this makes clear that it is not nearly enough to talk about individual rights. If we are to have communities, we must have group rights. The ultimate limit on the state is that it should not be able to stamp out whole cultures or to compel them to take on new forms. In Canada, we have tried, feebly, to entrench group rights in our constitution from the beginning; but the time has come when one must do a good deal more. Some representation in the system must be by cultural group and not simply by place.

As things stand now, a Francophone in Victoria is effectively disenfranchised on any question having to do with language and culture by the simple fact that he is hopelessly outnumbered. The long-term tendency has been for the Francophones, therefore, to gather in Quebec and northern New Brunswick — a tendency which, as I have suggested repeatedly, must be fatal in the long run. If, however, instead of our present well-loved Senate, we had an upper chamber of communities, Francophones, Anglophones and Native peoples might all be represented in ways which were not diminished by a tendency to dispersal. Whenever one suggests such things, the question arises: how shall we decide who belongs to what group and how shall we do it without creating a permanent ghetto? Everyone should be able to decide to which group he belongs just as citizens in Ontario now decide which school system they will

FÊTE DU PATRIMOINE
Lundi, 16 février, 1981

La fondation canadienne pour la protection du patrimoine
C.P. 1358, Succ. B, Ottawa, Ontario, K1P 5R4

Heritage Canada   Tom Wood, 1981

The wheat pool elevator stands as a symbol of our dream of the creation of new kinds of wealth designed so that one man will not be enriched at the expense of another. But if you look closely, you can still see the capitalist grain companies.

support with their taxes. Anyone is free to change from one group to another.

I doubt that there would be many such groups in the long run even if we set no limits on the number which could be established. Native peoples, the French and the English constitute founding groups. Other peoples came later and, with certain exceptions like the Doukhobors, knew full well that emigration entailed joining an existing culture.

But I see no reason why some Canadians should not seek to revive or continue Polish or Ukrainian cultures or should not, if they choose, decide to constitute a communal group for purposes of political representation. Ultimately, perhaps, criteria would have to be established to determine what might and might not constitute such a group; but it is not beyond the scope of the democratic process to make that decision. The long term tendency would perhaps be for people to orient themselves around one or other of the predominant cultures. Inter-marriage, for example, tends to move people toward the dominant culture.

I rather think that we shall need to go one step further if we really want our pluralism to have a firm base: we shall have to vest certain resources in such groups. There has been much talk and bitter argument in recent years over the ownership and control of natural resources such as oil. But much more important than these are resources which, at present, are hardly controlled at all. At one time clean air and clean water were taken largely for granted as, I think, sunlight still is. These resources must be protected both from pollution and from abuse by one cultural group attempting to dominate another. Any community must ultimately insist that such resources be used for the public good — that they not simply sit there being beautiful while men live in misery and poverty. Similar considerations ought to apply to oil, coal, water power and whatever other resources happen to concern us.

One possibility to meet these concerns is to attach the resources which are at present not clearly assigned to communal groups in such a way that one, say, who wanted to start a factory which had a bad effect on the air would have to pay a royalty to the groups to whom such resources were assigned. My proposal would be that the groups share the resources in proportion to the population of their members. Thus a person wishing to use the air would have to get the consent of the royalty holders. The holders would be groups and, on the whole they would have to agree with one another (though there would have to be a limit so that one isolated group could not prohibit all development). Out of the royalty, the groups would administer such measures as might be needed to restore the air quality. The rest of the royalties would accrue to the groups. But the funds would have to be used by the group as a group for the support of the group and not be distributed to individuals.

The result would be, of course, a disincentive to the misuse of such a resource, a fund which would tend to support communal groups, and a system within which, nevertheless, there would be some incentive to the actual and acceptable use of such resources.

I think some such creation of new kinds of property is inevitable. The most important question is whether it will be assigned (as most property now is) to individuals or whether it will be used to support group rights.

The example provides a framework within which we can look at existing property rights in conventional resources. The thesis is that they belong to the provinces but that the federal government, as things stand, can determine what happens by any number of means, chiefly taxes, tariffs, and export controls.

The system tends to absurdity: the short-term advantage is to use resources to the benefit of the present inhabitants of advantaged provinces. The ultimate absurdity must strike any of us who stops to think about it. I was born and grew up in British Columbia and now I live in Ottawa. Whatever share I might have had in British Columbia's resources I have presumably traded for an interest in Ontario's resources. But does buying a bus ticket to Vancouver make one a British Columbian and does walking accidently over the border into New Brunswick disenfranchise a native Québécois of his interest in Quebec culture?

All questions of division within a federation pose the same conundrums. If Albertans want to decide on the question of separation from the union, who is to decide? Those in Alberta this morning? Native Albertans wherever they live? All Canadians?

No answer makes any sense. But if no answer makes any sense, the resources are not divisible in the way that has been proposed. That seems to go for both sides. There is no more reason why the federal government should dispose of Alberta's resources than that Albertans should dispose of Alberta's resources; for there is a real chance that the federal decision will be made *entirely* by non-Albertans — if, for instance, no Albertans sit in the caucus of the majority party.

Where no answer makes sense, someone has asked the wrong question. The right question is not "Who owns the resources?," but "How can they be fairly distributed?"

Our history and philosophy suggest that it would make more sense if resources belong to the provinces in the plural, not in the singular. One could say, that is, that just as the "new resources" I spoke of might be owned communally — but jointly by the communities not singly by any community — so the provinces might own the resources jointly not singly. This would mean that they would have to agree on their use. We would not trade Alberta's oil for Quebec's hydro power; but both would have to sit down and decide how oil and water power *alike* could best be used for the common good. As Charles de Koninck never tired of saying, we cannot remind ourselves too often of the primacy of the common good.

One needs to ask, no doubt, just what it is that the provinces represent. For one thing they represent a second layer of the state which counteracts that "grand état" of which de Koninck spoke. And that is something in itself.

But they represent, of course, history and tradition and in some cases culture. It is banal to remind ourselves that this is truer in the Maritimes than in Alberta, but Alberta has its own history, its own outlook and its own traditions even if they are diluted somewhat by massive immigration. Our philosophers have all warned against cutting loose from history and tradition. We may well see a regrouping of provinces but there is no reason to suppose that we should or shall see their abolition.

Advantages, though, have their prices. Pitting the provinces against the centralist state has for its price that there is a body of provincial politicians for whom the balance of advantage lies in harassing the federal government. For without that, they are in danger of being assimilated to the federal structure.

Equally, keeping the provinces in their present form disadvantages large groups, especially Francophones across the country who, outside Quebec and New Brunswick, do not form a powerful enough group to be sure of a hearing though, in Ontario, they can be very useful to a political opposition — and so occasionally elsewhere.

If we really believe in bilingualism and we believe in maintaining the present provincial boundaries and structures, we shall have to take further steps. One of them I have already suggested —representation by cultural community in an upper chamber. But somewhere in Canada we shall have to have another major population centre in which people speak French. Along the railway from Quebec City to Prince Rupert there are French communities or remnants of them. Canada will have to have another major port on the Pacific and everyone knows that the economics of wheat shipment have made that an approaching reality. Why should not the new city be French speaking? Some might say that British Columbians would be outraged. I'm sure that at one time they *would* have been outraged. I'm not so sure that they would be now. After all, another answer is that it is not really in the interests of Quebec nationalists that such a possibility should be opened. Again, I think that this might have been true at one time and might easily be true again but we are living at a moment when, by a bare majority, Québécois have decided to live with confederation.

Such a city would displace no one (it will not be exactly on the site of the present Prince Rupert). It would give French culture access to the west, make possible the movement of French speakers beyond Quebec and it would give British Columbia not only access to a new culture but access to a whole dimension of traditional Canadian political power. Perhaps that is a mad dream but some time *some* such mad dream must become a reality. For nothing else will repair the damage done by the failure of Riel and the consequent closing of the west to the French-Canadian culture.

We must remind ourselves, however, that a powerful coherent culture within a larger community can easily become a ghetto. The *individual* right that it is most important to protect in a new constitution which recognizes group rights is the right to move from one group to another. Groups must somehow compete for members, not compete to exclude them. We have usually been able to cope with that problem in Canada but it would become much more pressing if group rights became a stronger reality.

Finally, if the state on *these* terms is to succeed, it must function as the coordinator of cooperation not as the enforcer of conformity. Thus the independence of the courts becomes more and more important. But so does the question of who becomes a judge. Lay representation even on the highest courts of appeal becomes essential for a society that departs from a competitive model. Our legal system will become increasingly complex, even if the state tends to 'wither away' as more subtle questions of justice arise. The more one relies on the courts, the more one must democratize them. In Canada, the jury system has grown gradually into a responsible and serious institution. The principle should be extended and, in higher courts, a combination of professional and lay assessors is both natural and realistic.

Clearly, we do need a new constitution. It needs to be rather unlike the one we have. But it is clear too that a new constitution need not represent a break with the past. We have time to evolve and we need neither lament nor panic.

Chapter 10

Not Like the Others

I began by remarking that the existence of Canada has always excited wonder. Indeed, in conventional terms, Canada, as a nation, is not possible.

Conventional wisdom has it that there have to be unifying forces to which one can point — one language, or one culture, or one clear geographic region. If you do not have a single language like the Germans, or a dominant culture, like the French, then you ought, like the Swiss, to have one kind of scenery and to have mountains and lakes for your borders.

Everyone knows that there are exceptions. But the life of Belgium rather resembles the *Perils of Pauline*. India is trying hard to forge a common language. Senator Hayakawa sees even a little bilingualism as perilous for the United States. The Russians, to put it mildly, try to have one ideology.

Canadians do not try. Divided by geography, unsure of what version of either official language they speak and write, proud of a culture in which any man may wear a tam o'shanter in any tartan of his choosing, they also like to frighten themselves by buying large numbers of strange books called things like *Bilingual Today, French Tomorrow*.

That, of course, is just the surface. Beneath the surface, there is a long history of common principles and outlooks and there is a common experience which has brought us together. It seems odd to follow Pierre Berton in saying that there would not have been a Canada if the War of 1812 had not brought us together, but it is true that, whenever some threat of assimilation from without or separation from within becomes sufficiently real, the common principles and the common experience come to the surface.

This is not enough to make a nation. To have a nation there must be a tendency toward a common strategy. But I think there is enough of that, too. Though, as I have been arguing, our economic strategies have been too superficial, our communitarian tendencies are apparent enough.

THE TORCH; BE YOURS TO HOLD IT HIGH!
IF YE BREAK FAITH WITH US WHO DIE
WE SHALL NOT SLEEP, THOUGH POPPIES GROW
IN FLANDERS FIELDS.

McCREA.

Public Archives (C87137)   R. Filipowski, World War II

And now the future: The art deco monuments look like model skyscrapers.
On one, figures seem to approach heaven via the Empire State Building. Is it
an accident that the torch bearer has turned his back on them?

If I am right, the concept of nation is the concept of the common outlook and strategy which is reflected in the way in which institutions display themselves. The institutions may, indeed, be legitimized by a variety of communities, each of which is anchored in its own culture. And the strategy adopted by a pluralistic nation will be one which encourages pluralism, just as its institutions will be responsive to all the communities which render them viable and legitimate.

The common confusion about the "nation" is the result, I think, of a tendency to think of the nation as if it were the community, or a culture, or some special institution (such as the state). Hence the tendency for communities and cultures to be homogenous is mistaken for some resultant necessity in the nation. Even "la patrie," the homeland, the place of one's origin is not the nation: we do not all, in Canada, have a *homeland* in the same sense, but we may well all be Canadians despite that.

The problem is just this: it is a perilous business running a nation which is not like the others. We do need to act collectively, for the principles which underly our union are threatened from all sides, not by the perversity of Americans, or Russians, or Englishmen, or Frenchmen, but by the very nature of the modern world. It is the tendency to a unified faceless culture based on some form of possessive individualism which makes our future one which requires a good deal of protecting.

We have looked at economic and political questions in their own right. In this chapter, my concern is chiefly with culture and it is very hard, in a pluralistic community, to know just how one should or could respond. It is sometimes alleged that we ought to have a great drive to create a dominant unitary culture. Such drives are not impossible. In a sense, the French had one after the Revolution, and it is the result of that which was deplored by Simone Weil in *L'enracinement*. Whether or not such a drive would be fruitful, the truth is simply that Canadians have little stomach for it.

On the other side, it is sometimes said that we should not do anything at all to defend the basis of our unity because anything which we do is likely to result in the creation of a forged identity so that we will henceforth go through life with moustaches and beards painted on our sombre faces, clutching documents fabricated by the Canada Council in lieu of the natural passports with which the others promenade across time. But the fact of the matter is that, though we do feast on bits of other people's cultures, especially on the crumbs and scraps of the intellectual fast-food business, we fear that we shall be malnourished and we *do* itch to intervene.

The first thing to remember, I would think, is that what the community feeds on is the culture. Culture includes everything which gives meaning to human actions, but the part of the culture on which we can *work* is the part which has to do with the creation of the objects in which we can find our own reflections and the part which has to do with the passing on of tradition.

It is our novels, our poetry, our paintings and our music which serve most easily to express to one another what we are. But there are many levels of this. It is important not just to support the most talented creators but also to see to it that it is possible for people to express themselves to each other. We have spent much effort creating a class of professional creators of culture — a class which tends to be drawn from the other professional groups. The professionals are the ones whose children see the importance of being a professional. But we have spent rather less effort in helping people from the more general public to establish their own identity.

Not only is this true. It is also true that our universities, the institutions which serve chiefly to guard tradition and to generate new knowledge, are mainly staffed by middle class men from middle class families who draw their students from their own environment.

In both these matters, we need to be more concerned about reaching into society and about seeing to it that what is there to be expressed does get into the open. Northrop Frye has spoken of the way in which folk tales may be transformed into myths and myths into literature so that one gradually builds a literature in which men can, at least, catch a glimmer of their identities and of their relations to each other. The principle which he has been concerned with applies, of course, not only to literature but to all art. The transformation of folk music, the transformation of religious images, the transformation, even, of the painting with which the cave man hoped to trap the spirit of the animal he sought, are all examples.

But the development of a culture depends on the constant iteration of the original process and on the development of the special abilities of some of those within that original structure. We have grasped the importance of this in our efforts to revive native arts, but we have not been so interested in the drawings of Cape Breton coal miners or the verses of British Columbia fishermen. We have, indeed, in reality, a long history of "people's art" — of an art which bears a real relation to the social situation of those whose lives modern technology has transformed. The interactions between the visual arts, the class structure, and the whole economic and social system are documented in Barry Lord's *History of Painting in*

Canada: Toward a People's Art. But such issues — like much of that art itself — have usually remained out of sight. They have not greatly concerned the art galleries or the minds of the 'artistic establishment.' Our public institutions which provide the training for those with unusual abilities have drawn too heavily on their own kind.

Similarly, if, as I have been arguing, philosophy is largely the business of replacing and reconciling conflicting intuitions by appeal to reason, then we need to know a good deal more about those original intuitions than we in fact do if we are going to generate a philosophy which is responsive to our needs.

We really *do* need, be it said, some national institutions which will help us to understand each other and to make something of our underlying unities. When the French first founded l'Ecole Normale Supérieure in Paris, every community was allowed to nominate students. They came — young students, a retired admiral, intelligent men of middle age. And they so frightened the authorities that the place was closed for a time. But eventually, it produced Bergson, Brunschvicg, Sartre, de Beauvoir, Aron, Weil, Derrida — the greater part, indeed, of the cast of the French intellectual life in our time.

It was not, alas, re-opened with its original plan for student admission. But we might try that, again, in Canada and we might try, too, the French rule which guarantees those who succeed best a place in the educational system for the rest of their lives. We need not fear that such a national institution would usurp the place of established ones or that allowing some scope for national institutions somehow trespasses on the rights which God and Queen Victoria bestowed upon the provinces. We can negotiate about who is to run such places if we do not assume that what belongs to the provinces collectively must always belong to them singly.

We also need to make sure that the Canadian traditions — in music, in literature, in philosophy, in the social sciences — are seriously pursued in every institution. It is not narrow-minded to insist that all those who teach in universities, work in our cultural institutions, and take part in our public services, have a thorough knowledge of the Canadian tradition in their own fields.

This sense of a national culture is capable, I think, both of binding us together and of recognizing the discreteness of our various communities. Through literature and art we can build a world which we can share. Indeed, the point of the arts, in a sense, is that they enable men to live more than one life — to live some lives directly and some vicariously — and to share one another's visions.

But, in sharing lives and visions, we do not *become* each other. On the contrary, as I have suggested, we create a context in which we can become distinct, in which genuine individuality is possible.

Matthew Arnold rightly thought that the only thing which would break down the class structure in England was a shared culture. It is also true that the only thing which can bring about an honourable distribution of power is the sharing of a culture in which political power and possessiveness are simply not recognized as values.

But one must not imagine that such a shared culture needs to be homogenous. Indeed, it is precisely in the acceptance of variance that one develops a culture in which power is not a value. For the acceptance of variance entails that the power to press others to conformity is not acceptable.

Nor must one imagine, however, that such a culture can develop successfully in a world in which democracy is confined to the polling station and absolute autocracy is the standard of the workplace, or in a world in which the culture officially recognizes the value of communities while insisting that only individuals can be represented.

We must, indeed, eventually decide what we want. Whatever it is, it will require some skill. In a pluralistic society, in a society which recognizes both communities and individuals, there is never an end to the tensions. But that should surprise no one.

Our official national game is lacrosse — a game of speed and agility in which at any moment the other side may reverse the tide. It is not, despite appearances, that form of football in which one side aims to push the other off the end of the field.

Notes

Notes

These notes together with the bibliography contain the necessary references to books, sources drawn upon, and authors mentioned. They also include a glossary of important (and possibly confusing) terms, and identify, where necessary, men and women mentioned in the text. (I do not suppose I can be of any help with such cloudy identities as those of Shakespeare and Mackenzie King, but whatever I thought might be helpful to the reader has been included.) Where dates of birth and death are not given, the person mentioned is a contemporary. The notes are listed here in alphabetical order and not at the bottoms of pages because I think they are easier to find this way unless the reader is the sort of fanatic who stops in mid-paragraph to examine the sources. This system also avoids a great deal of repetition. A large number of references to Louis Lachance, John Watson, and Karl Marx can thus be concentrated in one place and condensed to a small space. Words followed by the symbol * indicate a further entry. Fuller identification of books mentioned in the notes will be found in the bibliography.

Acton, Lord (John Emerich Edward Dalberg Acton, First Baron Acton) (1834-1902) on power and corruption: Acton was professor of modern history at Cambridge and a liberal Catholic. He remarked that "power tends to corrupt and absolute power corrupts absolutely" in a letter concerning the controversy over papal infallibility. See *Essays on Freedom and Power*.

Alienation, two forms of: Hegel*, in the *Phenomenology of Mind*, distinguished between *Entäuserung* — giving up, or parting with — and *Entfremdung* — estrangement. The first of these is the ordinary process in which one gives something of oneself to the world in work or in art or in friendship. The second results when what one has given is swallowed up so that one cannot find one's mark on the world and so loses oneself. Marx* kept the distinction in the *Paris Manuscripts*. No easy English equivalent of the distinction can be found and "alienation" has become a distracting element in the "newspeak" of our day. There is a good discussion in H.B. Acton's *The Illusion of the Epoch*.

American society, loss of confidence in leaders: The poll cited is reported in *Psychology Today*, October, 1980.

Anarchism: Literally, the doctrine that there need not be a ruler. There have been several forms of it. P.-J. Proudhon*, apparently the first philosopher to call himself an anarchist, thought that social order of a mutualist* kind was essentially natural to men and that the imposition of a "ruler", far from being a part of natural order, was a sign of a fundamental disorder which needed power to control it. Other anarchists —Kropotkin and Bakunin for instance — have been even more strongly communitarian. Individualist anarchism of the kind associated with Max Stirner (the pseudonym of Johann Kaspar Schmidt, 1806-1856), though it has caught the popular imagination, has had much less intellectual backing.

Antigonish movement: The movement organized chiefly at St. Francis Xavier University at Antigonish, Nova Scotia, for the support of the cooperative movement. The university has become a major world centre of that movement.

Aquinas, St. Thomas (c. 1224-1274): his idea of the common good: For Aquinas the supreme good is God, but men also seek, and properly so, the natural perfection of man. Each man has his part to play in the unfolding of Providence but so does each other man, and the common good entails as much as possible the natural perfection of all men. This natural perfection is given, above all, by the idea of reason. Reason itself is common to men and entails, for its working out, a community. Aquinas's moral theory can be found in a number of places, but is best understood in the context of the *Summa Theologica*. A good, brief commentary is F.C. Copleston, *Aquinas*.

Arnold, Matthew (1822-1888): Poet, essayist, school inspector. His views on culture* are found mainly in *Culture & Anarchy* (1869, 1875) restored to its original form (with the wit back in place) in the Dover Wilson edition, Cambridge, 1932.

Aron, Raymond: Contemporary French philosopher, historian, social critic and journalist. Frequent opponent of Jean-Paul Sartre.*

Atwood, Margaret: Contemporary Canadian poet, novelist and literary historian. *Survival*, her study of Canadian literature, shows, as does much of her work, some influence of Northrop Frye*.

Bennett, Arnold (1867-1931): British novelist best known for his writings set in the potteries.

Bentham, Jeremy (1748-1832): British philosopher, held that the good consisted of the production of the greatest happiness (conceived as pleasure) for the greatest number. Associated with J. S. Mill*. See D. Baumgart, *Bentham and the Ethics of Today*.

Bergson, Henri (1859-1941): Leading French philosopher of the inter-war years, philosopher of evolution and of the élan vital.

Berton, Pierre on the war of 1812: In *The Invasion of Canada 1812-1813*, Berton says "the war which was supposed to attach the British North American colonies to the United States accomplished exactly the opposite. It ensured that Canada would never become part of the Union to the South." He admits that the cause was never very popular, but he thinks it was the *myth* of the war which eventually had its effect.

Blewett, George (1873-1912): Canadian idealist* philosopher who taught in Winnipeg and Toronto. His *The Christian View of the World* (originally lectures at Yale) and *The Study of Nature and the Vision of God* set out a view of nature which emphasizes both its fragility and our obligations to it. It clearly reflects his youthful experiences in the west. His theology is an attempt to make Christianity intelligible to the modern mind and to found theology on experience. The discussion of St. Thomas in *The Study of Nature and the Vision of God* is one of the most sympathetic written in English Canada.

Boethius, Anicius Manlius Severinus (c. 480-524): His *Consolations of Philosophy*, written while awaiting execution, was one of the most widely read books in the Middle Ages and constitutes an important link in the transmission of the neo-Platonist tradition.

Bourassa, Henri (1868-1952): founder of *Le Devoir*, nationalist, member of the federal parliament (1896-1907 and 1925-35) and of the Quebec national assembly (1908-1912). He was an ardent churchman and a critic of individualism and of the capitalist theory of property but never very comfortable in any political organization or inclined to march in step with any organized movement. His social theories are chiefly set in pamphlets.

Brett, George (1879-1944): Canadian philosopher (British-born) who was a major influence on philosophy at Toronto for a generation, turning philosophy strongly toward historical studies. His insistence on the historical development of the state is typical (see his *Government of Man*). He thought mediaeval philosophy, however, essentially derivative. His own philosophical views and his ultimate theory of history remain, rather obscure.

Brunschvicg, L. (1869-1944): Perhaps the greatest of the French idealist* philosophers.

Bunyan, John (1628-1688): The places described in his *Pilgrim's Progress*, (1678-84) can all be identified in the Bedford region.

Burns, S.A.M.: Canadian philosopher, teaches at Dalhousie University. See his "Rights and Collectivities" (reproduced, unfortunately, only in abstract) in S.G. French, editor, *Philosophers Look at Canadian Confederation, La Confédération canadienne, qu'en pensent les philosophes?*

Character, national, of Canadians: In addition to the material cited in the text, see Arnold, Stephan J. and Barnes, James G. "Canadian and American National Character as a Basis for Market Segmentation" in *Research in Marketing*, Vol. 2, 1979, pp. 1-35. They cite a variety of additional literature.

Charbonneau, Jean (1875-1960): Canadian poet, literary critic, dramatist and philosopher. In *Des influences françaises au Canada* (three volumes, 1916-20) he speaks feelingly both of the decline of French thought, the continuity of the "latin tradition" and the innate power of Quebec society to continue that tradition.

Class War: The battle which, according to Marxists, is made inevitable by the association of the means of production (e.g., land in a feudal society, productive machinery in a capitalist society) with a given class whose interests are therefore set against those of the remainder of society. It is not caused by ill will or bad motives but simply by the nature of the means of production.

Clastres, Pierre: Contemporary French anthropologist and social critic. His studies, especially of native tribes in Brazil, led him to question the Marxist thesis about the development of tribal societies into industrial societies. See his *La société contre l'état*.

Communitarianism: The doctrine that men find their natural expression (and develop their individuality) in communities. Opposed on one side to individualism (the doctrine that only individuals matter) and on the other to collectivism (the doctrine that the collectivity is more important than the individual). Close to Proudhon's* mutualism* except that it tends to place more stress on the continuity and reality of the community.

Community: Essentially a group of persons capable of establishing and legitimizing institutions*.

Cornell University: American institution of higher learning, founded by Ezra Cornell at Ithaca, New York, and opened in 1868. Its first president was Andrew White, the crusader against theological influences on higher education. Jacob Gould Schurman* succeeded him and tried to make Cornell's promise of an institution where "any man could study any subject" a reality.

Creighton, Donald (1902-1979): Canadian historian chiefly known for his thesis about "the empire of the St. Lawrence" and for his insistence upon the existence of a continuing Canadian tradition. See, especially, *The Empire of the St. Lawrence*. He says, in

Towards the Discovery of Canada, "I take my stand not with the positivists but with the so-called idealists, such as R.G. Collingwood, Michael Oakeshott and my friend William Dray* of Trent University". It was while Dray (now at the University of Ottawa) was at the University of Toronto (where Creighton taught) that he was more than anyone else responsible for making the ideas of Collingwood intellectually respectable in Canada.

Culture: Essentially the set of meanings given to human behaviour. Two different cultures exist when the same behaviour is habitually taken by two different groups to have two different meanings. The relation to artistic and to philosophical culture of culture in general is that culture in these two earlier senses provides (along with religion) the general background against which meanings are understood. (The word culture originally is derived from a Latin word, *cultura*, having to do with working the soil. But cultivation, in this sense is, after all, not only the basic act of *imposing* one's meaning on the earth but one of the basic acts through which human behaviour becomes intelligible in a deliberate way.) For anthropological senses see David Bidney's *Theoretical Anthropology*. Other discussions in these notes will be found under Matthew Arnold* and T.S. Eliot*.

Delos, J.T. (1891-1974): Political and legal theorist, member of the Dominican Order. Delos taught at Laval University and in France at the University of Lille. His *La nation* is one of the most extensive works in the field.

Demers, Jerome (1774-1853): Canadian philosopher whose *Institutiones philosophicae* was a text widely used in Quebec for about twenty years prior to 1855.

Derrida, Jacques: French philosopher who teaches at the École Normale Supérieure*, noted for his attacks on the systematic tendency of philosophy to impose a perverse order on human thought.

Descartes, René (1595-1650): The "father of modern philosophy." He insisted that our immediate knowledge of ourselves is more certain than our knowledge of anything else but he also insisted that certain ideas are innate, that the existence of God can be proved, and that men share a common rationality.

Dictatorship of the Proletariat: Marxist doctrine concerning the state of affairs after the collapse of capitalism. Since there will be only one group (see class war*), that group, the proletariat, will dictate the state of affairs. But the period will be one of transition to communism. "Dictatorship" is not meant to indicate a period of repression.

Donne, John (1571-1631): English poet and clergyman. His claim that "no man is an island" and each is a part of "the continent" is stronger than the Aristotelean claim that we all share in a common nature. He means to assert the neo-Platonic doctrine that there is an ultimate unity of which the parts are, ultimately, only aspects.

Dray, William: Canadian philosopher of history, teaches at the University of Ottawa. His *Laws and Explanations in History* has been one of the most influential works in the field amongst English-speaking philosophers, especially in Britain and the United States. He sought consistently to defend the position that causal explanations in history do not rely on laws like those of physics and chemistry.

Doukhobors: Literally "spirit wrestlers". A Russian sect which traditionally denied all authority whether temporal or spiritual and was persecuted under the Russian Czars. Tolstoy played an important part in their coming to Canada in 1898-99 where they settled in different places before and after the turn of the century but, in the end, chiefly, in British Columbia.

Duns Scotus, John (1270-1308): English Franciscan philosopher who continued, in part, the Augustinian form of the neo-Platonic tradition. A subtle thinker, the word "dunce" is derived from his name. It was widely and wrongly believed that he asked how many angels could dance on the head of a pin. In an

Aristotelean age, his views on the ultimate unity of being had become hard to understand.

Dvorak, Antonin (1841-1904): His music, influenced by Smetana* reflects a sense of place and of the uniqueness of cultures, whether Czech or of the new world.

École Normale Supérieure de Paris: French institution of higher learning founded after the revolution to open education to the people. Admission is competitive and the school has produced many of France's best known philosophers in this century.

Ego: The "I" or "self" which knows. In Freud's psychology, the ego mediates between the Id* and the Superego*.

Eliot, Thomas Stearns (1888-1965): Anglo-American poet, playwright and essayist. The theory of culture to which I refer here is one which rests deliberately on a theory of social classes and one which sees the literary and other arts as something won with difficulty, and to be defended against the assaults of modernity. Eliot's main concern is with the protection of a Christian culture, but his theory confronts that of Matthew Arnold who saw culture as a joint venture of the whole community and its only hope of reunion. Similarly Northrop Frye sees the higher culture (as it were) as developing out of folk-tale, myth and public experience, and as needing to preserve its roots and illumine the lives on which it draws, with, in the end, the prospect of regaining lost identities in several senses.

Engel, Marian: Canadian writer. Her novel *The Glassy Sea* depicts middle class religious life in rural and urban Ontario. It is perhaps the best Canadian account of transitions in and out of "modernity".

Ewart, John (1849-1933): Canadian lawyer, historian and patriot. He insisted on a genuine independence for Canada.

Existentialism: A body of philosophical doctrines associated with the belief that, for man, "existence precedes essence" — i.e. that men do not have predetermined natures like cabbages but are free to create themselves. The doctrine is associated with Sartre* who, however, was himself always attracted to (but critical of) Marxism*.

Falardeau, Jean-Charles: Canadian sociologist. He has done extensive work on French Canadian Society and on the relations between literature and the imagination.

Fearn, Gordon F.N.: Canadian sociologist. His *Canadian Social Organization* contains one of the few studies of national character.

Freedom: The expression is confusing. Philosophers often distinguish between the power to do something (positive freedom) and the absence of restraint (negative freedom). Freedom is sometimes confused with "indeterminism" in the sense of chance. (But no one says he is free if "by chance" he falls out of the window.) Spinoza* thought one was free if one's actions were determined by one's nature. Hegel* thought one was free if one was able to do what his real nature demanded. Less confusingly, perhaps, one is free if and only if one has significant choice.

French Language, Concern About in France: The concern about the ability of the French language to hold its own in the world is documented in *Le Point*, Paris for 7-13 July, 1980. See also the discussion of the Basque language in *Language and Society*, No. 4, Winter, 1981, pp. 19-ff.

French Language, Use of by Scholars in Quebec: The Quebec government study showing the tendency to use English was reported in *Le Droit*, Ottawa, for December 3, 1980.

French languages, Regional: See the report in *Le Point*, Paris, 11-17 August 1980.

French Revolution, How Reported in Canada: There is a fascinating discussion in *Les origines de la presse au Quebec, 1760-1791* by Jean-Paul de Lagrave.

Freud, Sigmund (1856-1939): Founder of psychoanalysis. Our concern here is with his theory of history and his questioning of the scope of human reason. See his *Totem & Taboo, Civilization and Its Discontents, Moses & Monotheism*, and *The Ego and the Id*.

Frye, Northrop: Literary critic and theorist of the imagination, ex-principal of Victoria College, now Fellow of Massey College and University Professor at the University of Toronto. His theories centre on the notion that all literature fits together to form a unity and that the manner of its doing so forms the subject matter of a critical science.

Garneau, Francois-Xavier (1809-1866): Canadian historian. His *Histoire du Canada* is based on the idea that there is a French *people* whose development forms a continuous and intelligible history in Canada. His theories are associated with those of Michelet.*

Grant, George: Canadian philosopher, now at Dalhousie, best known for his critique of technological society and for his defense of the idea of a Canadian tradition in public life. He was influenced by Hegel* but, as his concern about the forms of industrial society grew, his tendency toward Platonism also grew (see his *Philosophy in the Mass Age*). Later, he was influenced by Simone Weil* and Martin Heidegger*.

Green, T.H. (1836-1882): English philosopher who insisted on the importance of positive freedom*. Critic of John Stuart Mill*.

Groulx, Lionel (1878-1967): Canadian historian and cleric. Major force in French Canadian nationalism.

Hegel, G.W.F. (1770-1831): German philosopher, most persistent modern critic of individualism and the most influential figure in the nineteenth century development of the idea of history and its importance in human affairs. Marxism*, Phenomenology* and numerous other movements are critical developments of aspects of his thought. Hegel believed that the rational was the real, that the history of western civilization was the history of the idea of freedom and that men ultimately formed a natural unity.

Heidegger, Martin (1889-1976): German philosopher and critic of technological society. He was concerned at modern man's rejection of being and ultimately believed that the whole history of western philosophy had taken a wrong turning in ancient Greece. He greatly influenced George Grant*.

Herbart, Johann F. (1776-1841): German philosopher who developed some of the foundations of the notion of the unconscious. One of Kant's* successors at Konigsberg.

Herridge, W.D.: Canadian minister to Washington during the regime of R.B. Bennett.

Hobbes, Thomas (1588-1679): British philosopher who thought that men were matter in motion, that they tended to eliminate one another, and that the life of man in the state of nature was solitary, poor, brutish and short. In his *Leviathan*, he proposed strongly authoritarian government.

Houde, Roland: Canadian philosopher who has made a particular study of philosophy in French Canada, has compiled a substantial bibliography of philosophy in English Canada as well, and who is a recognized expert on the work of Jacques Maritain.

Huxley, Aldous (1894-1963): English novelist and thinker. Critic of the industrial revolution.

Id: Literally the "it", rendered in German as "das es" and in French as "le ça" but used by Freud* to designate the impersonal forces in the human psyche.

Idealism: The word has many meanings in Philosophy. Subjective idealism (as in the philosophy of Bishop Berkeley) is the doctrine that nothing exists except the mind and its states or contents as known to the subject, while objective idealism is the doctrine that reality is a rational order. Platonic idealism is the doctrine that it is the forms or ideas — the archetypes of the world — which are finally real.

Idealism in Canada: The idealism which one finds in Young*, Watson*, Murray*, Blewett* and other Canadian idealists is always objective idealism (see above).

Ideology: A body of ideas which forms a basis for systematic human action.

Ideology, Marx's Theory of: On this view ideologies result from the idealization of social situations and frequently from history. For instance, "liberalism"* is an "ideology" on this understanding because it idealizes the freedom which certain people possess in a capitalist society and envisages a world in which everyone has the same freedom —forgetting that one can only be free in the way that a capitalist is free if there is another class.

Income distribution: The tendency for income distribution to worsen in the sense that the richest sub-group tends to get an increasing share of the total while the poorest sub-group gets a decreasing share appears to be quite common in western capitalist countries. The data, of course, are very complex and it should be remembered that the poor might be getting richer even though they were getting a smaller share of the total. The data for Canada are reviewed in *Reflections on Canadian Incomes* published by the Economic Council of Canada, Ottawa, 1980.

Innis, Harold Adams(1894-1952): Canadian social scientist whose work included a systematic attempt to reconceptualize the notions of time and knowledge and who studied political economy in the context of social history with particular emphasis on systems of trade and communication.

Institution: An organized body of human practices through which a community expresses itself. Hence we speak of legal, political, economic, religious institutions, and also, sometimes, of well-settled organizations with strong roots in the social order (e.g., banks) as institutions.

John the Scot (Johannes Scotus Erigena) (810-880?): Irish philosopher who settled at the court of Charles the Bald in Paris. He revived and developed the neo-Platonic tradition in Europe. His religious opinions were liberal (he thought that if anyone were in Hell God could not know it) and, after his return to England, he is said to have been stabbed to death by his pupils with their pens.

Kant, Immanuel (1724-1804): German philosopher who believed that morality was a matter of universal principle, that history was propelled by the "unsocial sociability" of men who could not live alone but who sought to dominate one another, and that men should always behave as members of the Kingdom of Ends*.

Keirstead, Wilfred Currier (1871-1944): New Brunswick-born Canadian social philosopher. He taught at the University of New Brunswick for 36 years and, with Schurman, Innis, and Ten Broeke, is one of a group of religiously liberal thinkers with Baptist associations who have strongly marked Canadian intellectual life. Keirstead served on a number of public commissions which investigated railroads, mother's allowances and minimum wages and developed a reflective theory of democratic participation in government. As a young man, he served in various Baptist churches and his sermons (many of them now collected in the U.N.B. archives) show a remarkable concept of liberal, rational religion.

Kingdom of Ends, the: Kant's* moral community of rational agents in which each treats the others as an end in himself and not merely as a means. The ideal relationship of moral agents in which each is perceived as unique and irreplaceable, and the timeless ideal against which actions are to be measured.

Koninck, Charles de (1906-1965): Canadian philosopher (born in Belgium), concerned with the idea of the common good and with re-humanizing the world left by modern science and technology. Strong supporter of the Church, an institution which he saw as a protection against this dehumanization.

Kuhn, Thomas: American philosopher of science who has insisted that science must be studied historically and in its social context.

Lachance, Louis (1899-1963): Canadian philosopher, member of the Dominican order, chiefly concerned with legal and political philosophy and with the philosophy of St. Thomas Aquinas*. He contributed markedly to the ideology of nationalism in French Canada.

Lamonde, Yvan: Canadian historian of ideas who has worked extensively on philosophy and its teaching in French Canada.

Leacock, Stephen (1869-1944): Canadian writer, imperialist, anti-feminist and humourist. His *Sunshine Sketches of a Little Town* contain amongst the best images of turn-of-the-century small-town Canada.

Lee, Dennis: Canadian poet, critic, publisher and social critic. His *Savage Fields* is one of the most far-ranging critiques of the contemporary human condition to appear in Canada.

Leibniz, G. (1646-1716): German philosopher whose *Monadology* is one of the sources of the idea of an unconscious mind and whose mathematical philosophy was one of the great formative forces on modern western thought.

Lenin, V.I. (1870-1924): Russian thinker whose long meditations were capped by a brief but busy political career. His critique of the state* is one of the most cutting in existence.

Liberalism: The doctrine that what matters most is the individual's freedom of choice. Usually combined with the notion that men, left alone, will create a just or at least a decent society.

Locke, John (1632-1704): English philosopher who thought, contrary to Hobbes, that men would rather sell things to each other than eliminate one another. His ideal social contract is one in which government is severely restrained, property is protected, and conditions of trade are encouraged. He was very influential on the founders of the American Republic.

Lodge, Rupert (1886-1961): Canadian philosopher, (British born) who believed that there was an irreducible plurality of philosophical systems.

Lord, Barry: art critic and museum curator, whose *The History of Painting in Canada: Toward a People's Art* seeks to develop a theoretical framework within which the development of art in Canada is related to social and economic structures.

Lower, A.R.M.: Author of some classic formulations of the "two solitudes thesis" and, more recently, creator of a systematic view of history expressed in his *A Pattern for History*.

Lyall, William (1811-1890): Canadian philosopher, born in Scotland, who tried to reconcile reason and emotion and who attributed much of political life to The Fall.

MacLennan, Hugh: Canadian novelist. His *Two Solitudes* is the source of the phrase which has passed into the language. Overall, his novels provide one of the best keys to our culture. The words "two solitudes" were taken from Rainer Maria Rilke: "Love consists in this, that two solitudes protect and touch and greet each other".

Macpherson, C.B.: political theorist at the University of Toronto. His *Political Theory of Possessive Individualism* sets a standard from which other critiques have departed at their peril.

Marx, Karl (1818-1883): Adopted much of Hegel's* theory of history but differed from him on the vexed question of the importance of ideas. According to Marx, it is the economic sub-structure which divides men into classes and determines the shape of the social order while, according to Hegel, the technology which structures the economic order is itself a set of ideas which interacts with the rest of the system. Hegel sees a dialectic of thought and action in which the ideas which dominate a given epoch interact with each other. Marx sees a dialectic of forces within the economic order. See also the notes under ideology* and surplus value*.

Materialism: Like "idealism"* "materialism" is a term with a variety of senses. In one sense a materialist is one like Democritus, or Epicurus, or Hobbes who thinks that the world is composed

of and only of material objects. In another sense, a materialist is one, like Marx*, who believes that ideologies* are appearances determined by economic forces. (Marx's companion and frequent co-author, Friedrich Engels, tended to combine these two views.) One difficulty is to decide what "matter" is supposed to be. Aristotle's matter was essentially the ability to take on form. The "matter" of Democritus (and Hobbes) consisted of lumps of hard stuff. Neither has much to do with the situation described by equations in modern physics.

Mathews, Robin: Poet, playwright, critic, and defender of the belief that there is a substantial and identifiable Canadian culture. Mathews is one of the few poets of our public life, and one of the principal forces behind the resurgence of cultural nationalism in the nineteen-sixties and nineteen-seventies.

McCulloch, Thomas (1777-1843): Canadian philosopher (born in Scotland), theologian, and story teller. Trained in medicine and languages and devoted to theological quarrels, he has a claim to be considered the first professional philosopher in English Canada.

McLuhan, Marshall (1911-1980): The man who warned us that the medium is (or at least might become) the message, used many of Harold Innis's* ideas but took them much further to make communications theory the basis of a critique of modern society.

Mennonites: Protestant sect, Swiss in origin, named for Menno Simons. The group was formed in Zurich about 1523 and spread to France, Holland and Russia. Mennonites have come to Canada from various places, many of the oldest groups coming from the United States at the time of the American revolution. They are pacifists, refuse oaths, and many sub-groups are opposed to various kinds of technology (including automobiles and some kinds of farm machinery), though there is no general rule about this in Mennonite doctrine.

Mental Patients, Treatment of: The discussion in the text is based on data from the American National Institute of Health and on public health statistics in Canada.

Merleau-Ponty, Maurice (1908-1961): French philosopher, perhaps academically the most respected of those associated with the phenomenological and existentialist movements in France. He succeeded Louis Lavelle in the chair which Henri Bergson had held at the College de France.

Metaphysics: Literally "that which comes after the physics", originally applied in the first century A.D. to Aristotle's thirteen books on "first philosophy"; the study of the ultimate nature of reality; an enquiry into such questions as whether there are minds, or only material objects, whether men are free and whether God exists. The "metaphysics of community" is concerned with such questions as whether only individuals exist or whether communities have a claim, as well, to be considered real, and also with questions about the bearing of doctrines such as materialism* and idealism* (in their different forms) on questions of political philosophy.

Michelet, Jules (1798-1874): More than anyone, the man who made "the people" the centre of historical studies (see his *Le peuple*). His *Histoire de France* appeared a dozen years before François Xavier Garneau's *Histoire du Canada*, and his influence is evident.

Mill, John Stuart (1806-1873): British philosopher, champion of liberalism (see *On Liberty*), of the doctrine that the good is to be assessed in terms of pleasure (see *Utilitarianism*) and that the promotion of pleasure for oneself and others is a duty.

Morton, W.L. (1908-1980): Canadian historian, a major force in shaping the writing of the history of the Canadian west and one of those most concerned with notions of national identity in Canada.

Mure, G.R.G.: Oxford philosopher whose *Retreat From Truth* provides one of the most trenchant criticisms of empiricism and its association with capitalism. An idealist, he is also a Hegel scholar of renown.

Murray, John Clark (1836-1917): Canadian philosopher (born in Scotland), best known for his work in ethics and philosophical psychology. He was also a social critic of force and pioneer spokesman for the education of women.

Mutualism: The doctrine of P.-J. Proudhon* that between individualism (the doctrine that only individuals matter) and collectivism (the doctrine that the collectivity is more important than the individual) there is the possibility that men must work together for their well-being. In a rough way, one may consider such a doctrine as slightly more individualist than the theory I have called communitarianism* in this book.

Myth: Most commonly a timeless story, widely told in a given culture, involving the supernatural and associated with basic understandings about how the world is. But the word is widely used with one or more of those elements missing. For instance, a story which simply reveals how a given people look at things is sometimes called a myth.

Neill, Robin: Canadian economist, teaches at Carleton University. He has done the best job with the difficult task of making Innis's economics systematically intelligible. See his *A New Theory of Value: The Canadian Economics of Harold Innis*.

Nozick, Robert: Harvard philosopher of the new right —takes a stronger view than Locke* of the association of natural rights and property.

Nation: Sometimes used as equivalent to "state" and sometimes as equivalent to "community". I have taken the view that the community is what legitimizes institutions and shows itself through them and that the state is just one of those institutions. We do need a word, however, for the collective principles and strategies to which the institutions give rise and, on historical and other grounds, I used "nation" here for this. In this sense, a theory of "the nation" is something we badly need and which this book only begins to develop.

National consciousness: The sense of conscious identity which those who shape and are shaped by "the nation" may have.

National identity: The set of ideas (mainly dispositional, i.e., not always conscious but likely to be evoked by various events) which forms the common character of those in a nation. In the Canadian case it has many elements, but one of them is the idea that plurality is a good thing and this gives a special and sometimes puzzling slant to the national identity.

Olive Trees, The Sacred: In Athens the olive tree was protected and one may find many trials of offenders for cutting down trees (even dead ones). The goddess Athena had given them to the city. See Kathleen Freeman's *The Murder of Herodes and other trials from the Athenian Law Courts.*

Obligation: Something one must do as a moral or legal duty. Philosophers debate sometimes the priority of rights* and obligations. Here I argue that our most basic rights derive from the fact that we must have certain freedoms in order to carry out our obligations as citizens.

Ouellet, Fernanrd: Canadian historian, teaches at University of Ottawa. Authority on social and ideological history of French Canada.

Pâquet, Louis-Adolphe (1859-1942): Canadian philosopher and cleric, a nationalist and very conservative churchman.

Patrie, La: Literally, the "fatherland" but, generally, the sense of a place where one belongs, has roots, and where the pattern of development is one which finds expression in one's own outlook. It may not be one's "nation"* and often is not one's "state"*, but it is apt to be associated with one's community* and culture*.

People's Bank, The: Institution opened by P.-J. Proudhon* in Paris, the aim of which was to provide capital at nominal interest rates for artisans since the artisan could not work without materials but could be set free if he had something to work his skills on. It was the prototype in practice of the credit union and the Caisse Populaire and, in ideology, a step toward the notion that a real bank is one in which each would deposit his talents and draw against them for his needs. Proudhon was imprisoned shortly afterwards and closed the bank for fear that it would not run well during his absence but, like many of its co-operative successors, it seems to have worked.

Phenomenology: Literally the science of "phenomena" or appearances but usually used for those philosophies which descend from Edmund Husserl, a German philosopher (1859-1938) who greatly influenced Sartre*, Heidegger*, Merleau-Ponty* and others and who sought to found a science on the correctly understood consciousness of the immediately given.

Plotinus (205-270): Founder of neo-Platonism. Believed in the ultimate unity of all things.

Pragmatism: Doctrine associated with the American philosophers Charles S. Peirce and William James to the effect that true propositions are those which are useful or solve problems. The philosophers concerned held it only with complex modifications but the word has passed into the language. Richard Nixon said he was a pragmatist.

Property: Something owned, or held to the exclusion of others. It is usually admitted that there must be property (even by Proudhon*) since some objects are useless unless their use and control can be predicted. (Scalpels for surgeons, beds, fountain-pens and motor-cars are like this.) The debate is over whether such things are held in trust for the community (even Locke* thought there was a residual public interest in all things) or whether some things can be owned outright, and over whether certain kinds of property (e.g. capital in a capitalist system) are by their nature socially destructive.

Proudhon, Pierre-Joseph (1809-1865): French printer-philosopher. Proudhon was the first philosopher to call himself an anarchist* but he meant the expression literally: he intended a world without a ruler, a natural community of honest men not pushed out of shape by arbitrary authority. He believed that a co-operative (mutualist*) economy would make such a world possible but he accepted that there would always be tensions in any human world, and rejected all those schemes (including Hegel's, though he admired Hegel*) which supposed a final resolution of the tension to be possible.

Psychoanalysis: Originally, the technique of Sigmund Freud for revealing the reality of the sub-conscious, now used for "depth" psychology generally.

Railways, grades on: It seems to have been common enough practice to build railways with a view to their use and so to set different grade limits for different directions. Albert Tucker in *Steam into Wilderness*, for instance, writes that, north of New Liskeard the chief engineer building the Ontario Northland recommended gradients at 26 feet to the mile rising north and 21 to the mile rising south. Presumably, heavy raw materials were to be brought south while lighter manufactured goods would be taken north. (These were "ruling grades"). The Grand Trunk Pacific — maximum grade .6 one way and .4 the other — is described by Nick and Helma Mika in *Railways of Canada*, Toronto, 1972.

Rationality: According to John Rawls*, a man is rational if he tries his best to further his own interests. (See *A Theory of Justice*.) Rawls says this is the common sense found in the social sciences. The older view deriving from Aristotle is that one is rational if one uses reason to control ones emotions and appetites. This suggests that rationality subordinates immediate self-interest to universal principle. Philosophers like John Watson* seem to have supposed that rationality consisted of acting universally — i.e. with the widest society imaginable as one's test for the interest to be served. Watson and Jacob Gould Schurman* held that reason itself is universal and knows no limits except those of knowledge and understanding. Hence it is generally the good of one's community (perhaps the nation) if not something larger that one seeks to serve. It is difficult to explain how rationality came to be confused with self-interest except perhaps through the idea of rationalization*.

Rationalization: Literally explaining away, making excuses for, frequently used by Freudians when they speak of making up stories to shield one from one's real motives. If, of course, it is rational to rationalize then rationality* may be associated with self-interest.

Rawls, John: Harvard philosopher who supports the social contract, ordered self-interest subjected to principles of fairness, and the thesis that one should choose that society which best advantages the least advantaged even if such a society depends on great inequalities of distribution.

Realism: The name of many unrelated philosophical doctrines: (1) the view that there are objects which exist independently of knowing minds (2) the doctrine that there are real universal ideas or Platonic forms (3) the view that universal optimism is not justified (4) the view that there are actual, particular material objects which scientific theories ought to describe (and others too numerous to describe here).

Regionalism, Frye's sense of: In *Aurora, New Canadian Writing 1980*, Northrop Frye* speaks of regionalism as a sign of maturity in culture. But the actual quotation suggests that by regional literature he means literature tied to a particular culture, so that any serious Canadian literature would be regional as opposed, say, to nurse fiction or stylized romances which are only vaguely associated with places and times. It is regionalism in this sense that he thinks is an antidote to shallow synthetic products of recent technology, but whether it needs to be tied specifically to Alberta or Newfoundland or might just be identifiably Canadian is a question which seems open to debate.

Richler, Mordecai: Canadian writer, winner of the Governor-General's gold medal. Perhaps the modern Canadian writer best known in Britain and the United States, he is noted for his descriptions of Jewish life in Montreal.

Rights: Legal or moral entitlements. They are generally associated with some obligation* (the obligation of others to honour them actively or passively) but whether they are tied to obligations in some stronger way is debated. It may be that the right to freedom of speech depends upon the fact that one has an obligation to one's fellow citizens to share in the structuring of the society.

Riesman, David: American sociologist, born in 1908, author of *The Lonely Crowd*, recently concerned with questions about the egotistical structure of American society. See his "Egocentrism" in *Encounter*, August-September, 1980, pp. 19-28.

Russell, Bertrand Arthur William (1872-1970): British philosopher. For something of his view of the relation between philosophy and culture see his *History of Western Philosophy and its Connections with Political and Social Circumstances from the Earliest Times to the Present Day*, London, 1940.

Sartre, Jean Paul (1905-1980): French philosopher, central figure in existentialism*, social critic with a strong interest in Marxism*.

Schurman, Jacob Gould (1854-1942): Canadian philosopher, born in Prince Edward Island, taught at Dalhousie, then went to Cornell* University where he became president. Later he was U.S. ambassador to Greece, China, and Germany. Developed a moral theory to mediate between Kant* and the social Darwinists. His theory of the state* is important but only sketched.

Smetana, Bedrich (1824-1884): Czech nationalist composer who greatly influenced Dvorak* and others.

Spinoza, Benedict (1632-1677): Dutch philosopher, much concerned with the ideas of rationality* and freedom*. See his *Ethics*.

State: Most commonly the political institution in a society as distinguished from the others (chiefly religious, economic, legal, and educational) so that one speaks of Church *and* State, education *and* the state, state control of the economy and so on. In Hegelian* usage, however, the state is distinguished from the institutions of civil society as final unification of individual and community. The ancient Greek state was a mystical union of men and their natural places, closer to "La patrie"* of modern usage. Lenin* thought that the state, by contrast, was merely a body of armed men having in their possession jails. It is the first sense — the state as one institution among many — that I use in this book. In this sense the state is a coordinating institution. If this is correct, would the state be needed if the other institutions were healthy and achieved their proper ends? *A* negative answer to this question would yield the orderly anarchy of P.-J. Proudhon*.

Stevens, H.H. (1878-1973): Canadian politician, founder of the Reconstruction Party, leader of the forces which compelled the Conservative Government of R.B. Bennett to enquire into combines and monopolies.

Superego: The force of conscience, presses the Ego from the side opposite the Id in the mythology of Sigmund Freud.

Surplus value, theory of: According to Marx* the source of value* is labour. But the labourer produces more than he earns. The economic system forces wages down (since business must be cost-efficient to survive) and there is therefore a surplus which accrues to the capitalist. The need to manage the surplus is at the centre of the problems of capitalism for it must be distributed, but cannot be consumed by labour within the terms of the system. Other factors (wages standardized by unions for instance) have intervened to take away the competitive advantage of low wages, but the system still tends to concentrate capital which must be invested, and it is the expansionary aspects of the system which often seem most troubling at present.

Sutherland, Ronald: Canadian literary critic strongly interested in the common features of French and English Canadian literature. See his *Second Image*.

Ten Broeke, James (1859-1937): Canadian philosopher, born in Vermont who taught philosophy at McMaster University from 1895 for 37 years until his retirement in 1932. He was a teacher of Harold Innis and a force for the liberalization of religion.

Tremblay Commission, The: Quebec Royal Commission of enquiry of 1956 into the constitution and the status of Quebec. Overall, it is the strongest account of the "dualist" position on Canada.

Trott, Elizabeth: Canadian philosopher, co-author of *The Faces of Reason*; authority on philosophy in English Canada, concerned with educational questions, broadcaster.

Value, instrumental: Something of value because it can bring about some change. Economics is concerned ultimately with instrumental values — the manufacture and exchange of goods and services. All instrumental values are concerned with changes in experience and anything, x, would have the highest instrumental value if it could change any specified experience into any other or retain any experience indefinitely. Marx thought that all such things could be represented as labour, as did Adam Smith. But this seems to be a mistake since labour is more or less efficient depending upon one social organization or another, and those social organizations can therefore be considered as instrumental values in themselves, as can anything (ideas, for instance) which plays a part in this process. It is possible to expand the idea of "labour" to include the making of social arrangements (e.g., getting married) or the occurrence of ideas (e.g., poetic insight) but it is not clear whether or not this leaves intact the idea of "labour".

Vanguard Party, the: Marx had urged that class consciousness was a necessary ingredient in the passage to communism and also that there would be a transition period called the dictatorship of the proletariat*. Marxists have argued as to whether or not there should be a conscious organization (the "vanguard party") to lead the way. The expression is ascribed to Lenin*.

Vico, Giambattista (1668-1744): Creator of the modern notion of historical development and critic of René Descartes*. Vico urged that history is the best real knowledge we have because we make history. Mathematics (he thought) consisted of inventions of our minds and was, therefore, something else which we knew for certain. Descartes had thought mathematics objective and history mainly speculative while mechanics or physics was our soundest science.

Viger, Jacques (1787-1858): Historian and antiquarian: a cousin of D.B. Viger (who played a large part in the events leading up to the rebellion of 1837 and was arrested but released), Jacques was elected mayor of Montréal in 1832 but devoted most of his life to the collection of historical materials. It was he who suggested the relation between Francois Xavier Garneau and Michelet and Proudhon. For an account, see Serge Gagnon, *Le Québec et ses historiens*.

Violence: Anything which forcibly disrupts the integrity of another. Derrida* has argued that even metaphysics can assault integrity and constitute a violence.

Watson, John (1847-1939): Canadian philosopher, born in Scotland, leading idealist, Gifford lecturer in Scotland, rival of Josiah Royce as the major philosopher of religion in turn-of-the-century North America. The views discussed in the text can be found in his *Outline of Philosophy* and *The State in Peace and War*. In his *The Christian Church in Canada*, H.H. Walsh ascribes to Watson a place in the ideological background to the creation of the United Church of Canada.

Weil, Simone (1909-1943): French philosopher, social critic and visionary. She gave up her job teaching philosophy to join the workers in the Renault factory and eventually died in England after playing a role in the French resistance movement. Her insistence on the primacy of obligation has interested philosophers like S.A.M. Burns*, and she was an important influence on George Grant*.

Wise, S.F.: Canadian historian of ideas, director of the Institute of Canadian Studies at Carleton University, has written extensively about the formative period of Canada after the American revolution and about the entrenchment of the idea of the organic society.

Woodcock, George: Canadian writer, born in Winnipeg and educated in England. Before his return to Canada after the Second World War he was an anarchist activist and editor of *Freedom*. In Canada, he edited *Canadian Literature* for a number of years. He has become increasingly interested in questions about federalism and political pluralism and with the variety of cultures in Canada. He has written books about Gabriel Dumont, the Metis leader, and about Indian cultures in British Columbia. He has written biographies of Orwell, Proudhon, and the American monk, Thomas Merton.

Young, George Paxton (1819-1889): Canadian philosopher and mathematician (born in Scotland) worked extensively in ethics but left relatively little published material.

Bibliography

CANADIAN PHILOSOPHY
: an historical-philosophical survey
by PROF. LESLIE ARMOUR
University of Ottawa

Thurs. Jan.19 12:40p.m. Rm.110 Lockhart

University of Winnipeg, Media Services   Thomas Morris, 1977

By 1977, Canadian philosophy was beginning to be a known subject matter.
But not without its puzzles, either. Eh?

Annotated Bibliography

Acton, H.B., *The Illusion of the Epoch,* London, 1955. Useful logical analysis of Marxism, but not very sympathetic.

Acton, Lord, J.E.E.D., *Essays on Freedom and Power,* ed. by G. Himmelfarb, New York, 1955. All power tends to corrupt and absolute power corrupts absolutely.

Albertini, M. et. al., *L'idée de nation,* Paris, 1969. Useful background.

Aptheker, Herbert, *Marxism and Alienation,* New York, 1965. Best collection of essays on a confused subject.

Aquinas, St. Thomas, *Summa Theologica,* tr. by the English Dominican Fathers, London, 1912-36. A clear, plain translation.

Artistotle, *The Politics,* tr. by B. Jowett, New York, 1943. An easy-to-read translation.

Armour, Leslie, *Logic and Reality,* Assen & New York, 1972. Explores the logic of dialectical systems and the relation of logic and metaphysics.

————— , *The Concept of Truth,* Assen & New York, 1969. Tries to explain why truth has a social context.

————— , *The Rational and The Real,* The Hague, 1962. What is it to talk sense in and about the world?

Armour, Leslie and Bartlett, E.T., *The Conceptualization of the Inner Life,* Atlantic Highlands, New Jersey, 1980: Analyses modern views of the human predicament.

Armour, Leslie and Trott, Elizabeth, *The Faces of Reason,* Philosophy in English Canada, 1850-1950: Waterloo, Ontario, in press, the only extended study.

Arnold, Matthew, *Culture and Anarchy,* ed. by H. Dover Wilson, Cambridge, 1932. Basic to any understanding of the idea of culture.

Atwood, Margaret, *Survival,* Toronto, 1972. Probably the most talked about view of the continuity of Canadian letters and culture.

Bailey, A.G., *Culture and Nationality*, Toronto, 1972. Useful and thoughtful essays by a pioneering Canadian social scientist.

Baumgart, D., *Bentham and The Ethics of Today*, Princeton, 1952. Frequently cited account of Bentham and his moral theories.

Berger, Carl, *The Sense of Power*, Toronto, 1970. A central reference point in recent Canadian intellectual history.

————— , *The Writing of Canadian History*, Toronto, 1976. Indispensible to an understanding of the Canadian taste for and in history.

Bergeron, Léandre, *Petit manuel d'histoire du Québec*, Montréal, 1970. Illustrates how history can be made the central feature of a cultural cause.
————— , *The History of Quebec, a Patriot's Handbook*, Toronto, 1971. Translation of above by Baila Markus and the author.

Berton, Pierre, *The Invasion of Canada, 1812-1813*, Toronto, 1980. Suggests the importance of the War of 1812 in the formation of a Canadian identity.

Bidney, David, *Theoretical Anthropology*, New York, 1953. Useful reference work.

Blewett, George, *The Study of Nature and the Vision of God*, Toronto, 1907. Shows evidence of friendly relations between Hegelians in English Canada and Thomists in French Canada.

————— , *The Christian View of the World*, New Haven, 1912. Reveals, amongst other matters, Blewett's concerns about nature.

Boethius, A.M.S., *The Consolations of Philosophy*, tr. by H.R. James, London, 1906. Best loved of the neo-Platonist works.

Bourassa, Henri, *Capitalisme, bolshévisme, christianisme*, Montreal, 1931. Bourassa's critique of capitalism.

————— , *Grande-Bretagne et Canada*, Montréal, 1901. Basic to the French view.

————— , *La langue française et l'avenir de notre race*, Montréal, 1913.

————— , *Le Canada, nation libre*, Montreal, 1926. Still worth thinking about.

————— , *Religion, language, nationalité*, Montreal, 1910.

Brett, George Sydney, *The Government of Man*, London, 1913. Strong historical emphasis.

Bunyan, John, *The Pilgrim's Progress*, 2 parts, 1678-84, ed. J. Wharey, Oxford, 1928.

Charbonneau, Jean, *Des influences françaises au Canada*, Montreal, 1916. Some curious and surprising views — but much serious thought, too.

Clastres, Pierre, *La société contre l'état,* Paris, 1980. Important anthropological critique of Marxism. Many suggestive ideas.

Copi, Irving and Gould, James, A., *Readings on Logic,* New York, 1964. Good on the importance of Hegel, provides much useful background.

Copleston, F.C., *Aquinas,* London, 1955. Best simple commentary.

Creighton, Donald, *The Empire of the St. Lawrence,* Toronto, 1937. The classic statement of the thesis about the river and the country.

————, *Towards the Discovery of Canada,* Toronto, 1972. These essays show more of Creighton's mind than any other writings.

Crowcroft, Andrew, *The Psychotic,* Harmondsworth, Middlesex, 1975. Good background to problem of mental disease, modern stress and medicine.

de Beauvoir, Simone, *The Ethics of Ambiguity,* tr. by B. Frechtman, New York, 1948. The basic account of existentialist ethics.

de Koninck, Charles, *The Hollow Universe,* Quebec, 1964. de Koninck's critique of the world of modern science and technology.

————, *Tout homme est mon prochain,* Quebec, 1964. Many subjects.

————, *Unity and Diversity of Modern Science,* Quebec, 1961.

de Lagrave, Jean-Paul, *Les origines de la presse au Québec,* Montreal, 1975. Mine of unusual information.

Delos, J.T., *La Nation,* Montreal, 1944. The biggest, most systematic study.

Demers, Jerome, *Institutiones Philosophicae,* Quebec, 1835. One of the best clues to philosophy in early to middle nineteenth century Quebec.

Descombes, Vincent, *Le même et l'autre,* Paris, 1979. Amusing and contentious study of philosophy in contemporary France. Important for a grasp of the importance of Hegel.

Donne, John, *Devotions Upon Emergent Occasions,* London, 1624. No man is an island.

Dray, William, *Laws and Explanations in History,* Oxford, 1957. Still the best statement of Dray's concerns about history.

————, *Philosophy of History,* Englewood Cliffs, N.J., 1964. Well-thought-of basic text.

Economic Council of Canada, *Reflections on Canadian Incomes,* Ottawa, 1980. The facts on the gloomy picture of income distribution.

Eliot, T.S., *Notes Towards the Definition of Culture,* London, 1948.

Engel, Marian, *The Glassy Sea,* Toronto, 1978. One of the best pictures of life and religion in middle class English Canada.

Ewart, John, *Canada and the British Wars,* Ottawa, 1922. Unsentimental straight stuff about us and the British.

Falardeau, Jean-Charles, *Imaginaire, social et littéraire,* Montreal, 1974. An important link between literature and the social sciences.

Fearn, Gordon F.N., *Canadian Social Organization,* Toronto, 1973. Rare discussion of attitudes and national characteristics.

Fedida, Pierre, *Dictionnaire de la psychoanalyse,* Paris, 1974. Best layman's guide to psychoanalysis.

Forsey, Eugene, *Freedom and Order,* Toronto, 1974. Our constitution as seen by *the* expert.

Freeman, Kathleen, *The Murder of Herodes and Other Trials from the Athenian Law Courts,* London, 1946: Crime in ancient Athens — and the matter of the sacred olive trees.

Freud, S., *Complete Psychological Works,* ed. J. Strachey et. al., London, 1953-64. The whole thing. The issues cited here are from *Civilization and its Discontents, The Ego and the Id, Moses and Monotheism and Totem and Taboo.*

Frye, Northrop, *Anatomy of Criticism,* Princeton, 1957. Frye's starting point.

———, *Creation & Recreation,* Toronto, 1980. Most recent account of the central myth.

———, *The Bush Garden,* Toronto, 1971. Frye's Canadian concerns.

———, *The Critical Path,* Bloomington, 1973. Best account of Frye's philosophical position.

———, *The Secular Scripture,* Cambridge, Mass., 1976. The other side of *Creation and Recreation.*

Gagnon, Serge, *Le Québec et ses historiens de 1840 à 1920,* Quebec, 1978. Vital for a grasp of Quebec and its attitude to history.

Galbraith, J.K., *Money,* Boston, 1975. Draws on Adam Smith, but good and clear.

Garneau, François-Xavier, *Voyage en Angleterre et en France dans les années 1832 et 1833,* Quebec, 1855.

———, *Histoire du Canada,* Quebec, 1845 et seq., Centrepiece of the great historian.

Grant, George, *English Speaking Justice,* Sackville, 1978. Grant on Rawls and much else.

———, *Lament for a Nation,* second edition, Toronto, 1970. Starting point of a great debate.

———, *Philosophy in the Mass Age,* Toronto, 1959. Grant on the modern predicament.

———, *Technology and Empire,* Toronto, 1969. The Great Lakes civilization dissected.

Green, T.H., *Prolegomena to Ethics,* ed. A.C. Bradley, Oxford, 1883. Green's basic philosophical position.

――――, *Works,* ed. R.L. Nettleship, London, 1885-88.

Groulx, Lionel, *Histoire du Canada depuis la découverte,* 2 vols., quatrième édition, Montreal, 1962. Groulx's central work.

――――, *La Naissance d'une race,* Montreal, 1919.

――――, *Constantes de vie,* Montreal, 1967. Groulx in reflective mood.

――――, *L'Appel de la race,* Montreal, 1922. The novel which Ronald Sutherland found racist (it deals with vexed questions of cultural inheritance)

Hegel, G.W.F., *Phenomenology of Mind,* tr. by J.B. Baillie, London, 1910. Hegel's basic view of man.

――――, *Philosophy of Right,* tr. by Malcom Knox, Oxford, 1942. A bit bombastic and confusing to the ordinary reader, but it contains Hegel's fundamental theory of the state.

――――, *Lectures on the Philosophy of History,* tr. by J. Sibree, London, 1857. Straightforward account of the most influential theory of history.

Hobbes, Thomas, *Leviathan,* 1651, ed. M. Oakeshott, Oxford, 1946. Man as matter and the war of all against all.

Houde, Roland, *Histoire et philosophie au Québec,* Trois-Rivières, 1979. Essays in aid of the establishment of a history and its context.

Huxley, Aldous, *Brave New World,* London, 1932. The conditioned world.

――――, *Brave New World Revisited,* New York, 1958.

――――, *Science, Liberty, and Peace,* London, 1947. A good look at technology and the human prospect.

――――, *The Perennial Philosophy,* New York, 1945.

Innis, Harold A., *A Plea for Time,* Fredericton, 1950. Innis on time and knowledge.

――――, *Political Economy in the Modern State,* Toronto, 1948.

――――, *The Strategy of Culture,* Toronto, 1952. Protecting ourselves with understanding.

――――, *Empire and Communications,* 2nd. edition revised and expanded by Mary Q. Innis, Toronto, 1972. One of Innis's most influential theses.

――――, "Minerva's Owl", *Proceedings of the Royal Society of Canada,* 1947. A great essay which hardly anyone understood.

――――, *Changing Concepts of Time,* Toronto, 1952.

――――, *The Idea File of Harold Adams Innis,* ed., Toronto, 1980. A mine of ideas.

Johnson, A.H., *Whitehead's Philosophy of Civilization,* Boston, 1958. A Canadian philosopher looks at Whitehead's attempt to understand civilization.

Kant, Immanuel, *Kant on History,* tr. by L. Beck, E. Fackenheim, & R. Anchor, Indianapolis, 1963. The important writings by Kant on history.

————, *Kant's Critique of Practical Reason,* tr. by T.C. Abbott, London 1873, Kant's important moral writings.

Keirstead, William C. "Ideals in Dictatorships and Democracies", *Dalhousie Review,* April, 1939.

————, Discussion in Democracy", *Canadian Forum,* March, 1939. The kernel of the New Brunswick philosopher's views on politics.

King, William Lyon Mackenzie, *Industry and Humanity,* Toronto, 1918, 1935, 1947. King on compromise in the class war.

Klinck, Karl, ed., *The Literary History of Canada,* second edition, Toronto, 1976. *The* reference work.

Kuhn, Thomas, *The Structure of Scientific Revolutions,* 2nd. ed., Chicago, 1970. Most influential recent work in philosophy of science — insists on the social context and historical process of science.

Lachance, Louis, *Le droit et les droits de l'homme,* Paris, 1958. One of Canada's most creative philosophers looks at the law.

————, *Nationalisme et religion,* Ottawa, 1935. Nationalism, Canada, and the French culture from a philosophical perspective.

Lachapelle, R. et Henripin, J. *La situation démolinguistique au Canada,* Montreal, 1980. The facts.

Lamonde, Yvan, *Historiographie de la philosophie au Québec 1853-1971,* Montreal, 1972, Bibliography, selections, information.

————, *La philosophie et son enseignement au Québec,* Montreal, 1980. A study in depth.

Laurin, Camille, *Le français, langue du Québec,* Quebec, 1977. The Parti Québecois' view.

Leacock, S., *Sunshine Sketches of a Little Town,* London, 1912.

Lee, Dennis, *Savage Fields,* Toronto, 1977. "Literature and cosmology" — a free-flowing look at the modern condition, drawing extensively on Martin Heidegger.

Leibniz, G., *The Monadology and Other Writings,* tr. by R. Latta, Oxford, 1898. Leibniz's basic work.

Lenin, V.I., *The State and Revolution,* Peking, 1970. The state as a body of armed men having in its possession jails.

————— , *Materialism and Empirio-Criticism.* Still the most far-reaching work of Marxist theory.

Levant, Victor, *Capital and Labour: Partners?* Toronto, 1977. The class war in Canada.

Locke, John, *Two Treatises of Government,* London, 1690. The clearest basis of modern liberalism.

Lodge, Rupert, *Applied Philosophy,* London, 1951. Philosophy in practice and the conflict of systems.

Lord, Barry, *The History of Painting in Canada: Toward a People's Art,* Toronto, 1974.

Lower, A.R.M., "Two Ways of Life: The Primary Antithesis of Canadian History", Canadian Historical Association, *Report of the Annual Meeting, 1943.* Classic statement of the two solitudes thesis.

————— , *A Pattern for History,* Toronto, 1978.

Lyall, William, *The Intellect, the Emotions and the Moral Nature,* Edinburgh, 1855. Common-sense, St. Augustine and an attempt to make peace between the emotions and the intellect.

Macdonald, John, *Mind School and Civilization,* Chicago, 1952. A Canadian's case against John Dewey.

————— , *The Expanding Community,* Toronto, 1944. The basics of democracy.

MacEachran, J.M., "Some Present-day Tendencies in Philosophy", *Philosophical Essays Presented to John Watson,* Kingston, 1922.

MacLennan, Hugh, *Two Solitudes,* Toronto, 1945. The solitudes in fiction — the source of the popular image.

Macpherson, C.B., *The Political Theory of Possessive Individualism,* Oxford, 1962. A tough line against a pervasive view. Best Canadian critique of official liberalism.

Mardiros, Anthony, *William Irvine, The Life of a Prairie Radical,* Toronto, 1979. Leftist ideas on the prairies.

Marx Karl, and Engels, F., *The German Ideology,* tr. by R. Pascal, New York, 1933. Basic accounts of Marxist humanism and the critique of ideology.

————— , *Capital,* tr. by S. Moore, E. Aveling, and E. Unterman, Chicago, 1904.

————— , *Economic and Philosophical Manuscripts of 1844,* tr. M. Milligan, London 1959: The Paris manuscripts — Marx in a liberal mood.

Mathews, Robin, *Canadian Literature, Surrender or Revolution,* Toronto, 1978. An uncompromising nationalist account of our culture and its crises.

McCulloch, Thomas, *Letters of Mephibosheth Stepsure,* Halifax, 1860. The rural idyll and its defectors.

McKillop, A.B., *A Critical Spirit, The Thought of William Dawson Lesueur,* Toronto, 1977. Texts and commentary by and about a thinking civil servant.

———— , *A Disciplined Intelligence,* Montreal, 1980. Excellent intellectual history of the Victorian era in Canada.

McLuhan, Marshall, *The Gutenberg Galaxy,* Toronto, 1962.

———— , *Understanding Media,* Toronto, 1964. The heart of McLuhanism.

Merleau-Ponty, Maurice, *Sens et non-sens,* Paris, 1948. See his view of Hegel.

Michelet, Jules, *Le Peuple,* Paris, 1846.

Mika, N. and Mika, H., *Railways of Canada,* Toronto, 1972.

Mill, John Stuart, *Considerations on Representative Government,* London, 1861. Mill on how democracy might work.

———— , *On Liberty,* 1859, Oxford, 1912. Liberalism undiluted.

———— , *Utilitarianism,* 1863, Oxford, 1912. Pleasure for pleasure's sake.

Morton, W.L., *The Canadian Identity,* Toronto, 1961.

———— , *The Kingdom of Canada,* Toronto, 1962. General views of one of our most influential historians.

Mure, G.R.G., *Retreat from Truth,* Oxford, 1958. Cutting assault on empiricism, capitalism, and recent philosophy by one of Oxford's best.

Neatby, H. Blair, *W.L. Mackenzie King, Vol. III,* Toronto, 1976.

Neill, Robin, *A New Theory of Value, The Canadian Economics of Harold Innis,* Toronto, 1972. Vital for any understanding of economics and value.

Nozick, R. *Anarchy, State and Utopia,* New York, 1974. The new right, intellectualized: A Harvard philosopher argues against the claim that the rich and the strong have a duty to look after the poor and the weak. A book for winners.

Ouellet, Fernand, *Histoire économique et sociale du Québec, 1760-1850,* Paris, 1966. A fundamental examination.

Peyrefitte, Alain, *Rue d'Ulm,* Paris, 1963. Accounts from many sources of L'École Normale Supérieure.

Proudhon, Pierre-Joseph, *La misère de la philosophie,* Paris, 1847.

———— , *Qu'est-ce que la propriété,* Paris, 1840. Most quoted of Proudhon's works.

———— , *Système des contradictions économiques,* Paris, 1846. A basic theory.

———— , *Idée générale de la révolution au XIXième siècle,* Paris, 1851.

Pâquet, Louis-Adolphe, *Études et appréciations,* Québec, 1918. The philosopher cleric in many moods on many subjects — including the philosophers in English Canada.

Rawls, John, *A Theory of Justice,* Cambridge, Mass, 1971. Rationality as the pursuit of self-interest, the social contract revisited, justice and fairness.

Richler, Mordecai, *St. Urbain's Horseman,* Montreal, 1971.

Robinson, H.L., *Canada's Crippled Dollar,* Toronto, 1980. The importance of independence and the myths of foreign investment.

Rolph, W.K., *Henry Wise Wood of Alberta,* Toronto, 1950. An account of the founder of the prairie wheat co-operatives.

Russell, B., *Power,* London, 1938. A cool look at the heart of evil.

Schurman, Jacob Gould, *Kantian Ethics and the Ethics of Evolution,* London, 1881. Kant updated, but morality vindicated.

————— , *The Balkan Wars,* Princeton, 1914. A theory of national history.

————— , *The Ethical Import of Darwinism,* New York, 1887. The errors of social Darwinism.

Shortt, S.E.D., *The Search for an Ideal, Six Canadian Intellectuals and Their Convictions in an Age of Transition,* Toronto, 1976. Conflicts of over empiricism and reason: A close look at some Canadian thinkers.

Smiley, Donald V., *The Canadian Political Nationality, Toronto,* 1967. A much referred-to work.

Spinoza, B., *Ethics,* tr. by W.H. White and A.H. Stirling, Oxford, 1927. The classic of rational determinism.

Stewart, H.L., "The Imperialist Faith as Seen in Canada", *From a Library Window.* Last looks of an old imperialist.

Sutherland, Ronald, *Second Image,* Don Mills, 1971. Concerns the relations of French and English literature in Canada.

Sylvestre, Guy, ed., *Structures sociales du Canada français,* Quebec, Toronto, 1966.

Tardivel, Jules-Paul, *Pour la patrie,* Montreal, 1976 (with notes and commentary by John Hare). The novel which sets out the views of one of Quebec's strongest nationalists.

Ten Broeke, James, *The Moral Life and Religion,* New York, 1922. Toronto, Macmillan, 1940. Innis's teacher at work.

Tremblay, Jean-Jacques, *Patriotisme et nationalisme,* Ottawa, 1940. An important work which makes distinctions often forgotten.

Tremblay, Marc-Adélard and Gold, G.L., *Communautés et cultures — éléments pour une ethnologie du Canada français,* Montreal, 1973. Some essential basic ideas.

Tucker, Albert, *Steam into Wilderness*, Don Mills, 1978. The railway north — making nature fit.

Vico, Giambattista, *The New Science of Giambattista Vico*, tr. by M. Fisch and T.C. Bergin, Ithaca, 1948. The beginning of modern philosophy of history.

Walsh, H.H., *The Christian Church in Canada*, Toronto, 1956. Sound general history. Mentions Watson.

Watson, John, *Outline of Philosophy*, 2nd. edition revised, Glasgow, 1898. Watson's most general account of his philosophy.

————— , *The State in Peace and War*, Glasgow, 1919. Basis of Watson's social and political theory.

Weil, Simone, *L'enracinement*, Paris, 1949.

Wise, S.F., "Colonial Attitudes from the War of 1812 to the Rebellions of 1837" in *Canada Views the United States*, ed. by S.F. Wise and Robert Craig Brown, Toronto, 1967. Indicates tradition of the organic society.

Wolfe, Morris, ed., *Aurora New Canadian Writing*, Toronto, 1980. Contains Frye on regionalism.

Woodcock, George and Avacumovic, Ivan, *The Doukhobors*, Toronto, 1968. Sympathetic account of the Doukhobors and their problems.

Woodcock, George, *Anarchism, A History of Libertarian Ideas*, Cleveland, 1962. The standard history.

————— , *Gabriel Dumont*, Edmonton, 1975. A look at the chance we missed?

————— , *Pierre-Joseph Proudhon*, London, 1956. A good sympathetic study.

————— , *Peoples of the Pacific Coast*, Edmonton, 1977.

————— , *Ravens and Prophets*, London, 1972. Some reflections on British Columbia and its peoples.